THE ORIGINS OF AMERICAN POLITICS

THE

CHARLES K. COLVER LECTURES

BROWN UNIVERSITY

1965

THE ORIGINS
OF
AMERICAN
POLITICS

by Bernard Bailyn

Vintage Books
A DIVISION OF RANDOM HOUSE
New York

for

LOTTE

PREFACE

THESE THREE ESSAYS, which were delivered in their original form in November 1965 as the Charles K. Colver Lectures at Brown University, mark the convergence of two separately undertaken efforts of historical interpretation begun almost a decade ago. The first was a study of politics in America before the Revolution. This was a subject, I found, that had entered into the historical literature in many ways but that remained nevertheless obscure—remarkably obscure when one considered the prominence, indeed the dominance, of politics in the historiography of eighteenth-century England. Where for a generation historians of eighteenth-century England had dealt familiarly with the details of party or faction, historians of eighteenth-century America had touched on politics only incidentally, and when they had, had conveyed to their readers only the sense of triviality and boredom so well expressed almost a century ago by a diligent graduate student at Johns Hopkins University, Woodrow Wilson, who went into his colonial history examination, he wrote, "crammed with one or two hundred dates and one or two thousand minute particulars about the quarrels of nobody knows who with an obscure Governor, for nobody knows what. Just think of all that energy wasted! The only comfort is that this mass of information won't long burden me. I shall forget it with great ease."[1]

The obscurity and apparent triviality of pre-Revolutionary politics seemed to me to result, first, from a lack of clarity in definition. Politics is not the same as government, though the two are of course intertwined. The history of government is the history of those formal public institutions and procedures that constitute the framework of legal authority. The history of politics is the history of the ways men have used these instruments of power, the history of the struggles for authority, hence of the rivalries, factions, and interests that swarmed through and about the agencies of government. Failing to conceive of the struggle for power in pre-Revolutionary America as in itself a distinct process, historians with rare exceptions have merged it on the one hand with the history of formal institutions, and on the other with the chronicle of public transactions.

But the obscurity of early American politics is not the result of a lack of definition and focus only. Politics in the colonial period is a subject peculiarly difficult to locate within the broader dimensions of American history. Just as governmental institutions in pre-Revolutionary America were part of a larger grouping of institutions

---

[1] Wilson to J. H. Kennard, Jr., Nov. 18, 1884, quoted in Hugh Hawkins, *Pioneer: A History of the Johns Hopkins University, 1874-1889* (Ithaca, 1960), p. 283.

centering in England, so the pattern of political activity in the colonies was part of a more comprehensive British pattern and cannot be understood in isolation from that larger system. But the political system of the mid-eighteenth century, unlike much of the governmental system, came to an end in the thirteen colonies in 1776; it has no climax in the state and national party politics of later periods of American history. There is, consequently, no obvious eventuality to point to, and as a result no self-evident, pre-established principle of relevance for the historian to bring to his work. Even within the pre-Revolutionary period itself there is no obvious trend of development. Though there are on the surface certain evidences of growing maturity and progressive approximation of modern forms, the story of politics in the colonial period is not that of a distinct evolution toward the modern world: the evidences of growing modernity are delusive.

With these considerations in mind I proceeded with the study of politics in pre-Revolutionary America. But while I was engaged in this, a second project intervened, which I originally undertook as a divergence: the preparation of an edition of pamphlets of the Revolution. This led, as I have elsewhere described, to a general investigation of the ideological origins of the Revolution, and in the end to the assertion that the effective, triggering convictions that lay behind the Revolution were derived not from common Lockean generalities but from the specific fears and formulations of the radical publicists and opposition politicians of early eighteenth-century

England who carried forward into the age of Walpole the peculiar strain of anti-authoritarianism bred in the upheaval of the English Civil War.[2] I found too—and at this point I began to note a convergence of the separate lines I had been following—that the configuration of ideas and attitudes I had described as the Revolutionary ideology could be found intact, completely formed, as far back as the 1730's; in partial form it could be found even earlier, at the turn of the seventeenth century. More important still, it became clear that these ideas, which would become the Revolutionary ideology, had acquired in the mid-eighteenth-century colonies an importance in public life that they did not then have, and never would have, in England itself. The problem no longer appeared to me to be simply why there was a Revolution but how such an explosive amalgam of politics and ideology came to be compounded in America in the first place, why it remained so potent through years of surface tranquillity, and why, finally, it was detonated when it was.

In this way I was led back to the subject of early American politics, but now with a specific question in mind: what differences were there between the political processes in eighteenth-century America and eighteenth-century England that could explain the significantly different receptions of the same political ideas? It was a question, I found, that immediately gave shape to the political data I had gathered. The invitation to deliver the Colver Lectures at Brown University offered an opportunity to bring these materials together—the ideo-

[2] Bernard Bailyn, *The Ideological Origins of the American Revolution* (Cambridge, 1967), pp. v-x.

logical, from the study of the Revolutionary writings and their antecedents, and the political—into a single brief statement of explanation. It is this statement, written out somewhat more fully than the original lecture form permitted, that appears in the pages that follows.

I am grateful to the faculty and students of Brown University for their kindness to me at the time these lectures were given. I wish to express my thanks especially to Professor Elmer E. Cornwell, Jr., Chairman of the Political Science Department, and to my friends in the History Department, William G. McLoughlin, John L. Thomas, and the late Klaus Epstein, for their warm hospitality.

Jane N. Garrett assisted me in combing through the vast bulk of eighteenth-century newspapers and pamphlets and in settling a number of specific questions that arose in preparing the manuscript. The various drafts were read over and commented on by John Clive and Lotte Bailyn; their criticism at every stage was invaluable. When I first undertook the study of early American politics I was aided by grants from the Rockefeller Foundation and the Center for the Study of the History of Liberty in America. I am indebted to both of those organizations, and to the staffs of two splendid libraries— the Widener Library, at Harvard University, and the Baker Library, at Dartmouth College—for help most generously given.

B. B.

CONTENTS

THE ORIGINS OF
AMERICAN POLITICS

SOURCES OF
POLITICAL CULTURE

THE POLITICAL and ideological background of the
American Revolution has been studied by more
people over a longer period of time than any other topic
in American history. But old historical problems do not
preclude new solutions: indeed, they require them, for
historical explanations are delicate contrivances, capable
of being fundamentally upset by small bits of information
and transformed by shifts in historians' angles of vision.
The history of the major lines of interpretation of the
Revolution and its background constitutes in itself an
important chapter in American intellectual history, and
it provides a natural introduction to a reconsideration of
the subject.

For the Revolutionary generation the dominant characteristic of the great events of the age was their heroic
quality: the resulting historiography was a "heroic" interpretation. Written during and just after the events
themselves took place largely by the victors as part
of the process of binding the victory down, of

securing it on a higher level than war and politics, it is highly personified and highly moral history. Its presumption is that things were in good and stable order until evil men, for evil reasons, undertook to change them; had such malevolence not interfered, the *ancien régime* would have continued as it was indefinitely. So Mercy Otis Warren in her *History of the American Revolution* heaped blame and abuse on Thomas Hutchinson: "Few ages," she wrote, "have produced a more fit instrument for the purposes of a corrupt court. He was dark, intriguing, insinuating, haughty, and ambitious, while the extreme of avarice marked each feature of his character . . . [He] diligently studied the intricacies of *Machiavellian* policy, and never failed to recommend the Italian master as a model to his adherents." Her brother James Otis, on the other hand, typical of the Revolutionary leadership, was the very opposite: "His humanity was conspicuous, his sincerity acknowledged, his integrity unimpeached, his honor unblemished, and his patriotism marked with the disinterestedness of the Spartan . . . In his public speeches, the fire of eloquence, the acumen of argument, and the lively sallies of wit at once warmed the bosom of the stoic and commanded the admiration of his enemies." So too Parson Weems, our greatest mythographer, saw the war won and the nation founded by the superhuman bravery and absolute rectitude of George Washington, whose virtues he enumerated as, "1. His veneration for the deity, or religious principles. 2. His patriotism. 3d. His magnanimity. 4. His industry. 5. His temperance and sobriety. 6. His justice, etc. etc."

Similarly, or conversely, the loyalist Peter Oliver wrote as a history of the Revolution a sketchbook of heroes and villains—villains like Otis, who ended, Oliver reported with satisfaction, "rolling in the streets and gutters, the laughing stock of boys and the song of the drunkard"—he was "a living monument of the justice of heaven"; like Samuel Adams, "so thorough a *Machiavellian* that he divested himself of every worthy principle and would stick at no crime to accomplish his ends"; like John Hancock, "as closely attached to the hinder part of Mr. Adams as the rattles are affixed to the tail of a rattlesnake"; or like Franklin who, brought up as a printer's devil, "by a climax in reputation . . . reversed the phrase, and taught us to read it backward, as witches do the Lord's Prayer."[1]

A generation later everything had changed. The interpretation of the Revolutionary movement then most in vogue was almost the reverse of what had preceded it. Now a dominant Whig explanation laid stress, not on the fortuitousness of personal heroism and villainy, but on the inevitability of the outcome, the feebleness of men's efforts to hold back the tides of destiny, and the certainty with which the present, at any given point, could be seen to have been an improvement on the past. So George Bancroft introduced Epoch 3 in his *History of the United States* with the following words:

[1] Mercy Warren, *History of the Rise, Progress and Termination of the American Revolution* . . . (Boston, 1805), I, 79, 85; William A. Bryan, *George Washington in American Literature 1775–1865* (New York, 1952), p. 93; Douglass Adair and John A. Schutz, eds., *Peter Oliver's Origin & Progress of the American Rebellion* (San Marino, 1961), pp. 36, 39, 40, 79.

The hour of the American Revolution was come. The people of the continent obeyed one general impulse, as the earth in spring listens to the command of nature and without the appearance of effort bursts into life. The movement was quickened, even when it was most resisted; and its fiercest adversaries worked with the most effect for its fulfillment . . . A revolution, unexpected in the moment of its coming, but prepared by glorious forerunners, grew naturally and necessarily out of the series of past events by the formative principle of a living belief. And why should man organize resistance to the grand design of Providence?[2]

But by the end of the century this view too had faded— had in fact joined the heroic interpretation in the gallery of historiographical bric-a-brac contemplated with detached curiosity by a generation of scholars devoted to the canons of methodical, if not scientific, inquiry. These professional scholars of the early twentieth century, intent on eliminating with cold blasts of *Wissenschaft* all incrustations of myth, fancy, and filiopiety, devoted themselves to establishing the story on a solid foundation of facts. The facts, properly marshaled, were to speak for themselves. But in the half century that has followed, the facts have spoken not with one but with several voices, and their message is still far from clear. For one group of modern historians the crucial background of the Revolution has been found in a succession of social struggles said to be traceable through the first three quarters of the century—struggles variously described: for some, a

[2] George Bancroft, *History of the United States of America* . . . (New York, 1883–85 ed.), IV, 3, 4.

struggle of the dispossessed against the property-owning and power-controlling classes; for others, debtors against creditors; for still others, coastal aristocrats against inland democrats. However defined, it was for them a deeply-lying social struggle that marked the political history of the mid-eighteenth century and that entered into the controversy with England; in the end it was this same, persistent social struggle that shaped the polity of the new nation.[3]

Concurrently with the elaboration of these views there developed another major line of interpretation, often presented in combination with accounts of social and economic conflict but essentially distinct from them. Since it is the leading explanation at present both of the original characteristics of American politics and of the context and background of the Revolution, I would like to describe it at somewhat greater length—and do so in the words of its most powerful proponent, Charles M. Andrews. By the early eighteenth centry, Andrews wrote in his influential *Colonial Background of the American Revolution*, every colony had a representative assembly elected under more or less popular suffrage.

In time these representative assemblies increased the number and scope of their powers . . . opposed the feudal and royal powers wielded by the executive part

[3] For an epitomization of this view, see Bernard Bailyn, "Political Experience and Enlightenment Ideas in Eighteenth-Century America," *American Historical Review*, 67 (1961–62), pp. 339–340; for an enumeration of the leading works of this school, see Jack P. Greene, "The Flight From Determinism . . . ," *South Atlantic Quarterly*, 61 (1962), 236.

of the government, and began to claim for themselves all the privileges and functions of the House of Commons in England . . . As time went on, the assemblies came to look on these rights and privileges as a part of their historical heritage, inherent in themselves as representative bodies of people . . . these assemblies were going far beyond their functions as provincial councils . . . There could be no compromise between the view of the highest executive and legal authorities in England, on one hand, that the colonial assemblies, after one hundred and fifty years of growth and experience, were still merely provincial councils, possessed of limited and inferior powers, and the view of the colonists, on the other hand, that their assemblies had all the privileges of the House of Commons and, with some limitations, all the powers exercised by the parliament in Great Britain. These differences were irreconcilable, and the significance lies not in the fact of the conflict between the executive and legislative branches of the government—that is as old as assemblies themselves and is always with us—nor in the fact that a monarchical form of government was arrayed against one that was popular in character, though this was one of the fundamental points at issue; but in the existence in every colony of a miniature house of commons which was exercising full powers over legislation, membership, and finance, and claiming legislative equality with the highest legislative body of the realm.

But few British statesmen and politicians understood this development, Andrews wrote, and those who did were unprepared to accept its implication "that the empire was not a single state made up of a mother country and her dependencies, but rather a group of states equal in status, with coordinate legislatures and a common king."

Political struggles in the mid-eighteenth century reflected this effort of local forces to dominate the local government, and when the issue was introduced in constitutional terms in the 1760's, the English government insisted formally on "colonial subordination and dependence in the interest of the trade and commerce of their own kingdom." The result was the American Revolution and the disruption of the British empire. In this view, therefore, the political background and deeper context of the Revolution lie in the "rise of the assemblies" in America, from their rudimentary origins to the status of full-fledged legislatures incapable of simple subordination to external political forces.[4]

The rise of the assemblies, like the presence of social conflict, is unquestionably a major fact of eighteenth-century history, and it has been examined with great thoroughness by a succession of accomplished scholars: most notably, besides Andrews himself, Herbert L. Osgood, Leonard W. Labaree, Lawrence H. Gipson, and most recently Jack P. Greene.[5] Historians generally

---

[4] Charles M. Andrews, *The Colonial Background of the American Revolution* (New Haven, 1924), pp. 36, 40, 41, 66.

[5] Osgood's reliance on this conception is evident throughout the four volumes of his *American Colonies in the Eighteenth Century* (New York, 1924–25): it is more directly specified in his "The American Revolution," *Political Science Quarterly,* 13 (1898), especially pp. 41, 54–55; Leonard W. Labaree, *Royal Government in America* (New Haven, 1930), chap. v; Lawrence H. Gipson, *The British Empire Before the American Revolution,* especially vols. XI and XII (New York, 1965); Jack P. Greene, *The Quest for Power: The Lower Houses of Assembly in the Southern Royal Colonies, 1689–1776* (Chapel Hill, 1963). See also, among the more specialized monographs on the same theme written under Andrews' aegis, Mary P. Clarke, *Parliamentary Privilege in the American Colonies* (New Haven, 1943).

agree that it is a major theme in the political history of eighteenth-century America and that it is a necessary part of any explanation of the background of the Revolution that may be given. But it is not a sufficient explanation. For, in the first place, it does not make the dynamics of the Revolutionary movement intelligible—it does not provide a basis for understanding what impelled it forward at the time and place it moved forward. It is equally applicable to the British colonies that did not revolt (for example, the West Indies) as it is to those that did. Indeed, both Andrews and Labaree in their descriptions of the rise of the assemblies treat the mainland and the Caribbean colonies as a single undifferentiated group: this pan-British view is central to the orientation of their work. The true culmination of the institutional development they describe lies not in its termination in the thirteen mainland colonies but in its fulfillment in the nineteenth-century British empire and the twentieth-century commonwealth.

A more important limitation is the fact that this institutional history is insensitive to what the Revolutionary leaders themselves explained as the background and causes of the events of the 1760's and 1770's and to what they professed to be their own motivations. When the Revolutionary leaders said that they were attempting to defend self-government and with it English rights protected by English law, that is duly reported. But when they said other things, less readily associated with our notions of proper constitutional argumentation—and especially when these other things appear to us to be extravagant,

rhetorical, and apparently far from the realit
time—these things are either ignored or written o.   ɪne
inflated propaganda common to all revolutionary, indeed
all political, movements. Yet this language, in all its
extravagance, is a key not only to the thoughts and
motivations of the leaders of the Revolution but to their
actions as well. We shall not understand why there was a
revolution until we suspend disbelief and listen with care
to what the Revolutionaries themselves said was the
reason there was a revolution. When we do, we shall
discover not only a new dimension in the history of the
Revolution, and not only a new dimension in the earlier
political history of the colonies, but also linkages among
hitherto discrete and separated phenomena of the eighteenth-century world which combine into a new and I
believe a more satisfying story of the whole than we have
hitherto had.

We shall have much disbelief to overcome. For what
the leaders of the Revolutionary movement themselves
said lay behind the convulsion of the time—what they
themselves said was the cause of it all—was nothing
less than a deliberate "design"—a conspiracy—of ministers of state and their underlings to overthrow the British
constitution, both in England and in America, and to
blot out, or at least severely reduce, English liberties.
This undertaking, it was said, which had long been brew-
ing, had been nourished in corruption—rank, festering
corruption, rising from the inmost recesses of the English
polity and coursing through every vein. What was happening to America through the 1760's, point by point in

the controversy with England, could be seen, by the end of that decade, as fitting a pattern of concerted malevolence familiar to every eighteenth-century student of history and politics. Britain, it was said, was following Greece, Rome, France, Venice, Denmark, Sweden—in fact almost the whole of continental Europe—from the liberty of a free constitution into autocracy, and the colonies, for reasons variously explained, were in the van. Individual details—Stamp Act, Townshend Duties, Boston Massacre, and ultimately and overwhelmingly the Coercive Acts—added up to something greater, more malevolent than their simple sum, which was finally and fully revealed in the substitution of military for civil actions in 1775.[6]

So it was commonly said. But by whom? It was said not merely by acknowledged firebrands like Samuel Adams (though why it should be casually assumed that he had a peculiar stake in revolution is not at all clear) but by every major leader of the Revolutionary movement in the years before Independence: by John Adams, continuously, elaborately, year after year from 1765 to 1775, in his private as well as his public writings; by the cautious, conservative lawyer, John Dickinson, even in his explanation of why he could not support independence in 1776; by Thomas Jefferson, whose Declaration of Independence epitomizes and summarizes all these claims, though in phrases so familiar to us that it is difficult to recall their meaning.

[6] For a full development of this theme and for substantiation of the statements in the two paragraphs that follow, see Bernard Bailyn, *The Ideological Origins of the American Revolution* (Cambridge, 1967), chap. iv.

Did these sensible, well-informed men really believe what they said? For modern historians, knowing so much more than did the average American of the eighteenth century about the realities of Georgian England, and sophisticated as we all now are in the arts of propaganda, the answer must, at first at least, appear to be No. But if this is our answer, there are disconcerting facts that must be accounted for. There is indisputable evidence that certain groups in England, by no means under the sway of American propaganda, had the same understanding of the events of the time as did these Revolutionary leaders. It appears, furthermore, that what the American leaders were claiming in the decade before Independence had been claimed by others before them, in England and in America, not once, not twice, on occasions of bitter controversy, but repeatedly, for a century or more. The ideas, the fears, the pattern of responses and expectations in public affairs revealed by the Revolutionary leaders before Independence prove in fact to have been built into the very structure of political culture in eighteenth-century Britain and America. And more than that: it appears that these fears, these ideas, deeply bred in the awareness of eighteenth-century Britons everywhere, had a peculiar relevance and force in the American colonies, for America's political world was different from England's in ways that gave these ideas a heightened meaning.

It is this, in the end—this bearing of certain eighteenth-century British political ideas on the realities of politics in pre-Revolutionary America—that provides the sufficient background for understanding why there was a Revolution. It is this mid-century configuration of politics in its broadest sense that I propose to discuss.

It is not a simple assignment. In the end I shall be satisfied if I do nothing more than convey a useful point of view, and illustrate certain connections among events that are not commonly related. But I intend to begin more boldly. Risking the fate of Thomas Prince, who began his history of New England with the creation of the world and never got beyond the year 1633, or of Franklin's friend James Ralph, who got so entangled in the preliminaries of his projected *History of England* that he produced an Introduction of 1,078 folio pages but not a word besides, I would like to start at the beginning —the logical if not the chronological beginning—and speak first of the intellectual environment of eighteenth-century politics, and, more generally, of the greater political culture of which it was a part. Then, in the second lecture, I would like to turn to the structure of colonial politics—that is, the system of formal and informal institutions, procedures, conditions, and pressures within which politics operated, and discuss this in the form of a comparison with the equivalent phenomena in England. Finally, in the third lecture, I would like to follow out the ramifications of the strange, disruptive yet fruitful interplay that took place in eighteenth-century America between ideas and expectations on the one hand and the facts of politics on the other.

The starting point is the intellectual environment of eighteenth-century politics, the culture of which it was a part. Eighteenth-century Americans had behind them a century, more or less, of their own history, and they were aware of distinctive characteristics of their own culture. But the most important, most fundamental and determinative, thing about them was that they were in culture British—not Americans yet, nor simply Europeans, but specifically British. We shall understand little about politics or society in mid-eighteenth-century America until we understand what this implies.

It implies, preeminently, a sense of triumphant but still very recent and incomplete emergence; of success after desperate years of public turmoil: success acclaimed though still not established beyond challenge, still vulnerable and sensitive to threats. The struggles of the seventeenth century, with their ideological agonies, their panics and confusions, lay behind eighteenth-century Britons, in England and in America, though their lessons, the conclusions drawn from those convulsive years, were imprinted on the glass through which they saw the world. Georgian England was still provincial, still—despite its new refinements in taste and manners and the new elegance of its material possessions—crude to the point of savagery, boisterous to the point of riot. Hogarth not Gainsborough was its true depicter. J. H. Plumb writes:

> The placid countryside and sleepy market towns witnessed rick burnings, machine-smashing, hunger-riots. The starving poor were run down by the yeomanry, herded into jails, strung up on gibbets, transported to the colonies. No one cared. This was a part of life like the seasons, like the deep-drinking, meat-stuffing orgies

of the good times and bumper harvests. The wheel turned, some were crushed, some favoured. Life was cheap enough. Boys were urged to fight. Dogs baited bulls and bears. Cocks slaughtered each other for trivial wagers . . . Death came so easily. A stolen penknife and a boy of ten was strung up at Norwich; a handkerchief, taken secretly by a girl of fourteen, brought her the noose. Every six weeks London gave itself to a raucous fete as men and women were dragged to Tyburn to meet their end at the hangman's hands. The same violence, the same cruelty, the same wild aggressive spirit infused all ranks of society . . . Young aristocrats—the Macaronis—fantastically and extravagantly dressed, riproared through the town, tipping up night watchmen, beating up innocent men and women. Jails and workhouses resembled concentration camps; starvation and cruelty killed the sick, the poor and the guilty . . . Vile slums in the overcrowded towns bred violent epidemics; typhoid, cholera, smallpox ravaged the land.[7]

Yet England was rich, and getting richer, her wealth "creating new standards of elegance and luxury for an ever-widening middle-class." And though France was still the great arbiter of fashion and the center of the cosmopolitan world in art and literature, and though the grand tour of the continent was still a necessary part of a proper education, England took pride in her achievements of mind and skill and imagination, and in her overwhelming successes in commerce and in war. Above all else, however, England prided herself on her success —a success that elevated the nation above all others, and most especially above France—in having established,

[7] J. H. Plumb, *Men and Centuries* (Boston, 1963), pp. 9–10.

after the upheavals of the seventeenth century, liberty as the principal goal of a stable and secure constitution.

It would be difficult to exaggerate the keenness of eighteenth-century Britons' sense of their multifarious accomplishments and world eminence and their distinctiveness in the achievement of liberty. From the end of the war in 1713 until the crisis over America a half-century later the triumph of Britain in warfare, in commerce, and in statecraft was the constant theme not only of formal state pronouncements and of political essays, tracts, and orations but of belles-lettres as well. There was a general paean of praise to the steady increase in wealth, refinement, and security, and to the apparent perfection in government. Even the poets bore witness to the dominant euphoria. James Thomson's finest achievement was *The Seasons,* but nothing interested him more than celebrating the triumphs and struggles of Britain, which he did briskly in *Britannia* (1729; his "Rule Britannia" would appear in 1740) and interminably in *Liberty* (1735–36), a vast autobiography of the goddess of that name which details the long history of her ancient greatness, her decline in "Gothic darkness," and her ultimate revival in Hanoverian England. An atrocious poem, it is nevertheless in its encapsulation of the national mood mingling pride, jubilation, and anxiety, and in its fusion of a hundred literary, historical, and graphic sources of political ideas and attitudes, one of the most revealing ideological documents of the age.[8]

[8] The ideological importance of the poem, to be discussed in more detail below, is brought out in Alan D. McKillop's monograph, "The Background of Thomson's *Liberty," The Rice*

But there were many like it in the flood of what has been called "Whig panegyric verse" that poured from the presses from 1700 to 1760 and that echoed from the stage in play after play in the early eighteenth century. No writer, however famous or obscure, could afford to neglect the theme of British liberty and power. Addison portrayed the trials and victories of liberty and public virtue in his immensely popular and influential play *Cato* (1713), while in the same year Pope concluded his *Windsor Forest* with a vision of a triumphant Britain bringing peace to all the world. And if Edward Young's *The Merchant. An Ode on the British Trade and Navigation* is a minor poem of a minor poet it nevertheless develops in its celebration of commercial success a motif characteristic of the thinking of the age.[9]

Institute Pamphlet, XXXVIII, no. 2 (July, 1951). McKillop has edited, with commentary, both *Britannia* and "Rule Britannia," in *The Castle of Indolence and Other Poems* (Lawrence, Kansas, 1961). Cf. John E. Wells, "Thomson's *Britannia* . . . ," *Modern Philology,* 40 (1942–43), 43–56. For citations of Thomson in the literature of the American Revolution, see Index listing in Bernard Bailyn, ed., *Pamphlets of the American Revolution,* I (Cambridge, 1965); and also, e.g., the quotation from *Liberty* in [William Hicks], *Considerations upon the Rights of the Colonists to the Privileges of British Subjects . . .* (New York, 1766), p. 23n, and the paraphrase of "Rule Britannia" ("Ne'er shall my Britons or their sons be slaves") and the direct quotation of a stanza of the poem itself ("those beautiful lines of Mr. Thomson") in Alexander Martin's *America. A Poem . . . To Which is Added, Liberty. A Poem. By Rusticus . . .* ([Philadelphia, 1769?]), p. 7.

[9] C. A. Moore, "Whig Panegyric Verse 1700–1760," *Publications of the Modern Language Association,* 41 (1926), 352–401; Bonamy Dobrée, "The Theme of Patriotism in the Poetry of the Early Eighteenth Century," *Proceedings of the British ʾademy,* 35 (1949), 49–65; John Loftis, *The Politics of ʾma in Augustan England* (Oxford, 1963).

Poetry is too concentrated and refined a form, however, to convey fully the dominant self-admiration of Augustan England. The vulgar forms—the pamphlets, treatises, periodicals, and newspapers: the teeming political literature of the day—express it more directly, and convey with particular clarity the specific political responses of the time. What they agreed on—even the doubters and Cassandras who will particularly concern us—was that England, as the once skeptical Montesquieu admitted by 1731, was "the freest country that exists in the world."[10] This belief was shared by every commentator of the age; it became one of the universal presuppositions of the century, on the continent as well as in England. So in far-off Vienna, Mozart's librettist has the captured Blonde in the opera *The Abduction from the Seraglio* resist her Turkish guard with the indignant cry, *"Ich bin eine Engländerin, zur Freiheit geboren!"* as if the mere identification would protect her against tyranny.

There was a broad core of affirmative belief universally shared by all informed Englishmen—shared even by those whose fears for the future would, in America, become the language of revolution. England's freedom, it was generally agreed, was directly attributable to its constitution of government, a constitution which better than any other known to history had harnessed the use of power. There was no mystery about how this had been managed. The pure forms of government—a classification conveyed from Aristotle by Polybius and Cicero, thence

[10] Montesquieu, "Notes sur l'Angleterre," *Oeuvres Complètes,* Édouard Laboulaye, ed. (Paris, 1875–79), VII, 195.

to seventeenth-century England by a score of Renaissance intermediaries—were monarchy, the rule of one; aristocracy, the rule of a few; and democracy, the rule of many or of all. All three forms in the course of history had degenerated repeatedly into their evil counterparts: tyranny, oligarchy, and ochlocracy or mob rule, which led ultimately to dictatorship and tyranny. But some success, it had long been noted, could be achieved by mixing elements of these pure forms within a single constitution so that the counterpoised pressures generated by the three acting upon each other might keep the system stable and healthy.

The value of such a balance was commonly endorsed by sixteenth-century writers, and in the early seventeenth century it came to characterize the working of the English constitution. English public institutions, it was observed, fitted very well the pattern of mixed government: an element of monarchy in the hereditary crown; an element of aristocracy in the House of Lords; and an element of democracy in the House of Commons.

Fusing traditional political theory, the medieval sense that the components of a polity were not people but estates or communities, and the particular institutions of the English government, the idea that England's was a mixed government gained currency through the sixteenth century and entered directly into the central flow of English political thought in Charles I's *Answer to the XIX. Propositions of Both Houses of Parliament* (1642). From this pronouncement—"one of the most influential ever made on the nature of the English government"—can be traced, through all the vicissitudes of the Civil War and Restoration, through the later Stuart challenges and the Glorious Revolution, the conviction that lies at the heart of English political thought in the eighteenth century: that liberty had been preserved and could be preserved indefinitely into the future by maintaining the balance in government of the basic socio-constitutional elements of society: king, lords, and commons.[11]

It is a simple notion, but easily misunderstood, for it naturally verges toward, and in part merges with, a different triad with which we are more familiar, that of functioning branches of government: executive, legislative, and judicial. The theory that the separation of functioning branches of government was a liberty-preserving condition had long been known in England. In partial form it had been a popular doctrine among the extreme radicals during the Civil War; Locke had discussed it (though for him the elements were different); and Montesquieu may have this primarily in mind in his famous discussion of the English constitution in *The Spirit of the Laws*. But while the concept of the separation of functioning branches had entered into the political literature, since 1660 it had been almost completely absorbed into the idea of mixed government. It was the latter and not the former that Englishmen most commonly pointed to as the heart of their constitution; it was this that they read into, if not in,

[11] For a full account of the history of the concept of mixed government in English thought, see Corinne C. Weston, *English Constitutional Theory and the House of Lords, 1556–1832* (London, 1965); the quotation is on pp. 23–24. For a classic statement of the theory in its early eighteenth-century form, see *The Spectator*, no. 287 (Jan. 29, 1711/12).

Montesquieu; and it is this primarily they believed they saw demonstrated in the political stability of their time.[12]

It was this balance, they believed, that had eliminated from England that perennial curse of government, arbitrary power. Executing the law was, to be sure, the crown's prerogative, but the crown was checked in this role by courts controlled by aristocratic and popular elements; and in the making of law—so the theory ran—the crown participated as one of three equal components. So too the aristocracy in the House of Lords, selected, Blackstone said, "for their piety, their birth, their wisdom, their valor, or their property,"[13] participated as a part of the legislature in making law and as the highest appellate court in interpreting it, but was constrained by the other orders to which it was yoked from capturing the whole of government. And the commons, or "the democ-

[12] For an excellent discussion of the seventeenth-century origins of the idea of the separation of functioning powers and of its subsequent absorption into the concept of mixed government, see W. B. Gwyn, *The Meaning of the Separation of Powers* (*Tulane Studies in Political Science*, IX, New Orleans, 1965), chaps. iii–vii. See also Bailyn, *Ideological Origins*, chap. iii, n.16. Gwyn's analysis of the confused relationship between the two concepts in the thought of Bolingbroke and Montesquieu is especially valuable. The distinction is easily blurred, in part because in actual operation mixed government necessarily involves the separation of functioning powers, the first estate's essential role being the exercise of executive authority. Perceptive commentators in the mid-eighteenth century recognized the logic of this overlap though they seldom explored the distinction as such: see, e.g., Hume's essay, "Of the Independence of Parliament," in Charles W. Hendel, ed., *David Hume's Political Essays* (New York, 1953), especially p. 69; and William Blackstone, *Commentaries on the Laws of England*, I, 155.

[13] Blackstone, *Commentaries*, I, 50–51 (cf. I, 157–158).

racy"—that is, the distinct part and only that part of the population denominated "the people"—expressed its separate and unique interest, liberty, in its law-making role in the House of Commons, and as a participant in the court system defended its rights against the excesses of executive power. Yet "the democracy" too was kept from overwhelming the constitution; it was constrained by the energies of the two other orders, which shared interests (power, order, stability, hierarchy) antithetical to the special interest of "the democracy."

This interpretation of the British constitution was widely popular in the late seventeenth century; it was universally accepted in the early eighteenth century. With its reinforcement in Montesquieu's *Spirit of the Laws* (1748) and its ultimate apotheosis in the first volume of Blackstone's *Commentaries* (1765), it became so pervasive as to constitute less an idea than a reflex. As such it colored all aspects of political and constitutional thought.

Yet as a description of the actual working of the English government it was not merely inaccurate but profoundly misleading. The balance of these elements —indeed, their very existence as distinct entities—was, if apparent, unreal. The supposed preserves of each power were in fact thoroughly infiltrated by the others, and the functioning of their roles was far otherwise than described. The nobility scarcely existed as a separate socio-constitutional entity; it acted not as a community with distinctive interests but as a group of individuals with myriad involvements, some enmeshed with and dependent on those of the crown, some part and parcel of "the democracy." Nor was the commons more discrete and unified an interest. It operated legislatively and judicially with elements of both the aristocracy and the crown in such a profusion of varying combinations as to defy description in these terms. And the crown, acting through its chief officers of state, far from being distinct in interest from the Commons and the Lords and no more than an equal co-partner with them in the legislature, operated with elements of both in both Houses to achieve in effect a mastery of the whole government which it maintained with rare interruptions through the century.

The source of the harmony and political stability of Hanoverian England lay not in the supposed balance of these socio-constitutional orders but in two sets or groups of conditions, the one underlying, the other manifest—both relevant, in ways that shall appear, to the form that politics would take in colonial America.

(I) Of the underlying elements, the first and most basic was the fact that the two great controversial issues of the seventeenth century—the extent of crown authority and the relationship of church and state—had been settled; settled in compromises, it is true, but compromises generally accepted throughout the realm. The King retained great powers. The administration of the government was still in his hands; ministers of state were still thought of as his servants, taken into government to serve his will; and the whole force of executive government remained his prerogative. But in the settlement reached after the Glorious Revolution he had sworn to govern according to the statutes of Parliament, and it was understood, at least after 1707, that the King would not veto acts of Parliament; he had given up any claim to the right to create courts by his own fiat or to dismiss judges without formal impeachment; he had agreed to convene Parliament at least once in every three years and to call for general elections at least once in every seven; not to levy taxes save by Parliamentary grant; not to maintain a standing army in peace time; and not to wage war for alien territories without the consent of Parliament. So too in religion a generally accepted compromise had been reached. The Church of England was established; it enjoyed the privileges and benefits of the state, and all who did not explicitly reject it were considered to be members of its community. But the traditional effort to identify society completely with the established church and to compel uniformity was abandoned. Dissent, at least by trinitarian Protestants, was tolerated, though penalized. The great majority of nonconformists were permitted to worship as they pleased, at first privately, then publicly. They enjoyed almost complete civil equality with members of the Church of England, and gradually in the course of the century attained a significant degree of political equality as well, in fact if not in law.

This settlement of the great questions of civil and ecclesiastical affairs was reinforced in its stability by two other underlying conditions. Government in eighteenth-century England played, and was expected to play, only a very restricted role in society. John Brooke, analyzing the role of parliament in the mid-eighteenth century, writes:

The idea that Parliament should enact a legislative program each session was completely unknown: legislation, when necessary, was conceived of as supplementing the existing common and statute law and bringing it up to date . . . The work of the British Government was virtually restricted to preserving the constitution (which meant doing nothing in home affairs) and conducting foreign policy.[14]

There was no expectation that government would act on society, especially on sensitive issues of society only recently laid to rest, unless forced to do so in anticipation of civil strife or in an effort to restore order once it was disrupted; and this presumption was realized in the generally quiescent attitude of both the administration and Parliament throughout the century.

Finally, there was the deep-lying sense, tending further to secure settlements once reached and to bind together community and state, that the officers of government, both of central government and of local, were entitled to the power they enjoyed; that they belonged in seats of authority not merely because they exercised authority with reasonable skill and restraint but by virtue of their birth, their material stake in society, and their personal accomplishments made possible by wealth, education, and leisure. Eighteenth-century England was governed by an aristocracy, but it was a successful aristocracy in that it was felt to justify its authority by the quality of its rule, and in this way perpetuated and reinforced the

[14] Sir Lewis Namier and John Brooke, *The House of Commons, 1754–1790* (London, 1964), I, 183, 184.

ancient assumption, still very much alive in the eighteenth century, that superiority should be unitary, that leadership in politics should fall to the leaders of society—natural leaders, leaders in status, in wealth, and in the skills associated with a superior style of life.

(II) Such were the underlying conditions of England's political stability in the eighteenth century. On the surface of public affairs a different set of conditions operated with the same general result. A system of accommodations had been reached between the two great political institutions in the nation—the crown, actuated in the ministry, on the one hand, and on the other, the House of Commons, now independent of the crown for its existence, legally by virtue of the Triennial Act, practically by virtue of the crown's financial need to convene it annually.[15] Conflict was built into their relationship, for unlike the sixteenth century, when the crown was the superior, and unlike the nineteenth century when the Commons attained supremacy and the crown was reduced politically to the role of mouthpiece for the majority leadership, the eighteenth century was a time of unstable

[15] The details that appear in this paragraph and the one that follows are derived from Betty Kemp, *King and Commons, 1660-1832* (London, 1959). For other presentations of the same theme, which apply to the earlier eighteenth century the mode of analysis Namier applied to the early years of George III's reign, see Brooke's "Introductory Survey," in *The House of Commons*, cited in the previous note; J. H. Plumb's *Sir Robert Walpole* (London, 1956-) (note especially the section on crown patronage in vol. I, 71ff.); John B. Owen's penetrating analysis of the fall of Walpole in *The Rise of the Pelhams* (London, 1957), pp. 37–40; and the classic earlier statement by William Holdsworth, "The Conventions of the Eighteenth Century Constitution," *Iowa Law Review*, 17 (1931–32), 161–180.

relationships; there was no automatic integration of these two authorities. The crown, indeed the King himself, was expected to be active in government, and he had great personal and institutional authority; but so too did the Commons. Harmony, or at least a working relationship between the two, was achieved by a series of conventions, unarticulated by, unknown to, the formal constitution of government. These conventions or accommodations, achieved by the use of what was called, technically, "influence," comprised in effect a private, informal constitution. Initiative was taken by the administration with the aim of extracting from the Commons compliance with at least its minimum wishes. It succeeded in this almost continuously throughout the century, in part because of the natural propensity of the independent county members of Parliament to support the administration and in greater part because of the government's careful manipulation of the votes of the borough representatives. This management, this successful manipulation of "influence," reached into the election procedures by which members were selected. Some boroughs—twenty-five or thirty—were owned outright by the government in the sense that a majority of their electorates were officeholders who could be dismissed if they opposed the government; in others the election of members favorable to the government could be assured by the proper application of electioneering funds. Beyond this, control of the House was assured by the distribution of the crown patronage available to any administration and by the management of the corps of placemen that resulted. In the middle of the eighteenth century about 200 of the 558 members of the House of Commons held crown places of one sort or another, and another 30 or 40 were more loosely tied to government by awards of profitable contracts. Of those who held places, 40 at least held offices intimately involved in the government and were absolutely reliable. The other 160 held a variety of sinecures, household offices, pensions, and military posts which brought them well within the grasp of the administration but yet required constant solicitation and management. A fluctuating number of other members were bound to the government less directly, particularly by the gift to their nominees of one or more of the 8,000 excise offices available.

On the surface, such influence over elections and such powers of patronage would seem invincible weapons for any administration seeking to control the Commons. But in fact control was always problematic and had always to be actively sought. At any given time seventy per cent of the placemen had received their places from the hands of a previous administration whose members may or may not have continued into the present one. The so-called Place Acts, especially that of 1707, while flatly barring from the House only a limited category of office-holders, required re-election of all members who accepted office from the government, which not only increased the expense of managing the House but led to an average loss of seven per cent of the members affiliated with the government. Finally, however unlikely, it was always possible for the government to be defeated at the polls and for even so skillful a Parliamentary manager as Robert Walpole to be forced out of office by opposition within the House.

The use of "influence" in managing elections and in controlling the houses that were elected was the key to the surface stability of government through the long transitional period between the age of monarchical control of government and that of the undisputed dominance of the House of Commons.[16] Certain technical preconditions were necessary for such an accommodation, and in passing we must note them, for their absence in America proved to be of the greatest importance. There must be patronage in abundance; the franchise must be limited, for the larger the voting population the greater the government's difficulty in controlling elections; representation must not be systematically related to the growth of and shift in the population; and finally, representation must be virtual rather than actual: that is, representatives must not be closely bound to the wishes of their constituents, but must remain susceptible to pressure from the government. All of these conditions existed in England in

16 So, among contemporaries, the conservative Hume saw it, writing in his essay "Of the Independence of Parliament," that "the crown has so many offices at its disposal that, when assisted by the honest and disinterested part of the House, it will always command the resolutions of the whole, so far, at least, as to preserve the ancient constitution from danger. We may therefore give to this influence what name we please; we may call it by the invidious appellations of *corruption* and *dependence*; but some degree and some kind of it are inseparable from the very nature of the constitution and necessary to the preservation of our mixed government." Hendel, *Hume's Political Essays*, p. 70.

the eighteenth century; all of them would disappear there in the course of the nineteenth century as the political system gradually changed into its modern form.[17] None of them existed in anything like the same measure in the mainland colonies of North America.

It was by these means and as a result of the conditions that stability in public life was maintained in Britain. It was a notable achievement, admired throughout Europe. Yet paradoxically, and for our purposes most significantly, the administrations that created this stability were the objects of ferocious, ideologically charged op-

[17] On the emergence of these elements in the origins of the eighteenth-century stability, see J. H. Plumb, *The Growth of Political Stability in England, 1675–1725* (London, 1967), a book of great relevance to the present discussion but which came to hand only after these pages were written. Professor Plumb's analysis of the late seventeenth-century instability and of the complex process by which England attained its famous eighteenth-century stability lends particular support to the present interpretation of the instability of eighteenth-century American politics. For he too finds a broad franchise, an insufficiency of crown patronage, and regular representation to be major elements of political instability and sees the creation of a new configuration of politics under Walpole in terms of the elimination of these conditions. On the breadth of the franchise and its meaning in late seventeenth-century politics, see pp. 27, 29, 34–35, 40, 41, 46–47, 55, 94–96; on the role of patronage and "influence" in the growth of political stability, see pp. 52, 60, 82, 96, 99, 109–127, 161, 166, 172, 179, 188–189; on representation, p. 39. For an analysis of the disappearance, in the early nineteenth century, of the pattern whose origins Professor Plumb traces, see Archibald S. Foord, "The Waning of 'The Influence of the Crown,'" *English Historical Review,* 62 (1947), 484–507; for a summary and interpretation, see Sir Lewis Namier's Romanes Lecture, "Monarchy and the Party System," reprinted in *Personalities and Powers* (London, 1955).

position, and none more so than the most stable administration of them all, Robert Walpole's (1721–42). Seldom in history has so secure and benevolent a regime been so viciously and continuously beset by opposition, so plagued by widely publicized suspicions of its motives, so ridden by anxiety. Walpole studied the opposition press with morbid concentration, and spent money left and right to buy up critical journals, establish favorable ones, bribe opposition writers, and hire others for the government. He was endlessly absorbed in dealing with opposition, forever alert to the possibility that some new combination would overthrow the government. When news of a Jacobite plot broke in 1722 he was not at all surprised, his biographer, J. H. Plumb, tells us:

Jacobitism obsessed him. He saw it everywhere. Just beyond his grasp the conspirators were at work. Jacobite agents lurked in the most unlikely places. Every suspicion, every hint needed to be tracked down. No informer was too corrupt to believe. Any ne'er-do-well, any cheat or double-crosser was sure of a careful hearing at Chelsea . . . Year after year Walpole built up a vast web of counter-espionage with his own spies in all the capitals and ports of Europe. The scantier the evidence, the more certain Walpole was; any measure was justified in bringing conspiracy to light. He could cross-examine for hours on end. He could countenance any gaoler's tactics, short of torture, if evidence might be forthcoming. The mere scent of a plot had been sufficient to excite Walpole to a restless, thrusting activity.[18]

[18] Plumb, *Walpole*, II, 41.

Yet Walpole was no neurotic. "No man ever was blessed with a clearer head," the faithful Lord Hervey wrote without exaggeration, "a truer or quicker judgment, or a deeper insight into mankind; he knew the strength and weakness of everybody he had to deal with, and how to make his advantage of both . . . no man ever knew better among those he had to deal with who was to be had, on what terms, by what methods."[19] If Walpole was obsessed by the fear of conspiracy, threats of conspiracy existed. "Right-wing"—Jacobite—conspiracies and threatened *coups d'état* of various kinds had in fact been common throughout the recent history of England. Everyone in politics in the early eighteenth century could recall that the late 1670's, with the Popish Plot, the impeachment of Danby, and the Exclusion Crisis that followed, had been a time of subversion and incipient rebellion.[20] And

[19] John, Lord Hervey, *Some Materials Towards Memoirs of the Reign of King George II* (Romney Sedgwick, ed., London, 1931), I, 17, 18.

[20] If a single short period of years is sought as the seedbed of the eighteenth-century ideology—a time when the elements of the later configuration can be seen converging for the first time into what would become a familiar pattern—it is undoubtedly the 1670's and early 1680's. (See, on this dating, J. G. A. Pocock, "Machiavelli, Harrington, and English Political Ideologies in the Eighteenth Century," *William and Mary Quarterly*, 3d ser., 22 [1965], 558ff., especially 565; and B. Behrens, "The Whig Theory of the Constitution in the Reign of Charles II," *Cambridge Historical Journal*, 7 [1941–43], 42–71.) These were years in which England was obsessed with conspiratorial fears, when "the existence, and practicability, of a design for the subversion of the Protestant religion was generally suspected" and when the uninformed and credulous of all classes (who were the majority) "readily believed absurd tales of large Papist armies, mysterious movements by night, secret papers scattered in the highways, of projected invasions from France and even from Spain. The wildest rumors swept the nation. Fires were

then within a decade, following Monmouth's Rebellion, had come the conspiratorial designs, as they were popularly understood, of James II, which had necessitated the *coup d'état* of the Whigs and William III known to history as the Glorious Revolution. And that was not the end. After the wild political gyrations of Queen Anne's reign, in which Whig politicians were impeached for treason and Marlborough's officers cashiered for the subversiveness of their politics, the defeated Tories fled abroad, contributing new forces to the expatriate groups known to be plotting the overthrow of the Hanoverian-Whig regime. The Jacobite uprising of 1715 only dramatized dangers generally felt, for "the Jacobite party in Britain was but one element of an extensive network of conspiracy that spread out over western Europe from the Boyne to the Danube." The renewal of the effort in another form in Atterbury's conspiracy of 1722, which pitched Walpole into a frenzy of counter-conspiratorial activity, evoked in some the fear that "a universal plot some time or other will unhinge all" or that England would soon end up in the hands of a military dictatorship.[21]

confidently attributed to Papist incendiaries unless clear proof existed to the contrary. A flood of pamphlets, many written by informers, stimulated fears . . . [in] the fevered imagination of the time." J. R. Jones, *The First Whigs: The Politics of the Exclusion Crisis, 1678–1683* (London, 1961), pp. 20, 22. Cf. Plumb, *Growth of Political Stability,* pp. 140–141, 149, 151, 152, 157.

[21] Archibald S. Foord, *His Majesty's Opposition, 1714–1830* (Oxford, 1964), p. 82 (see also, on the fears and activities of *coups d'état* in this "age of political conspiracy," pp. 51, 70–92, 106, 108, 129, 147); Robert Viscount Molesworth to John Molesworth, October 20, 1722, Historical Manuscripts Com-

The fact that a Jacobite uprising could be repeated yet again, twenty-three years later, in 1745, however hopeless that effort may have been from the start, testifies vividly to the realism of Walpole's concerns.

But the fear of conspiracy had other, subtler, and more deep-lying sources than these. It was generated not only by the activities of extremist "right-wing" forces known to be seeking the reversal of the Revolution settlement and hence of the whole constitutional structure of the state, but also by the activities of quasi-constitutional opposition groups, led, often, by members of Parliament, who accepted the Revolution settlement as such but objected strenuously to the uses that had been made of the government by those who had gained control of it.

One naturally tends to underestimate the importance of the opposition of the mid-eighteenth century, especially the opposition during Walpole's regime, for politically it was weak to the point of debility. Composed of a heterogeneous cluster of malcontents drawn from every segment of the political spectrum—from the far left, the inheritors of seventeenth-century libertarianism, as well as from the far right, ex-Jacobites and ex-Tories now undistinguishable from the centrist Whigs—it only rarely approached substantial voting strength in Parliament, and only once, when it forced withdrawal of Walpole's hated excise of 1733, in effect defeated the government. Yet as the

mission, *Report on . . . Various Collections,* VIII (London, 1913), 350. "By 1688," Professor Plumb writes, "conspiracy and rebellion, treason and plot, were part of the history and experience of at least three generations of Englishmen." *Growth of Political Stability,* p. 1.

amalgam known as the "country" interest, in contrast to the "court" interest of the administration and its supporters, it contributed powerfully to the sense of conspiracy that infused the political culture of Georgian England.[22]

It did so—despite its numerical insignificance, its instability, and its weak organization—in the first place because of the difficulty in the early eighteenth century of conceiving of sustained opposition to constituted authority as anything other than the work of parties, which, however benign in their origins, were believed naturally to degenerate into conspiratorial juntas whose aim in the end could only be the overthrow of the existing government. Parties, to almost every political writer of the early eighteenth century, were indisputably evil. The ancient ideal of an organic polity whose parts, operating independently within their assigned spheres, fitted together harmoniously, persisted. The King, it was universally allowed, made national policy and chose ministers as his servants to execute it, and the King would do no wrong; active opposition to the King's government, therefore, could only be a design to impose upon the King, and was hence improper, unconstitutional, and if persisted in, seditious. Party rivalries signified illness within the body politic, malfunctions within the system, not because all interests

[22] On the opposition under Walpole, see, besides Plumb's biography of Walpole, Charles B. Realey, *The Early Opposition to Sir Robert Walpole, 1720–1727* (Philadelphia, 1931); Foord, *His Majesty's Opposition*, chaps. i–v; and Kurt Kluxen's study of Bolingbroke's political thought, *Das Problem Der Politischen Opposition . . . im 18. Jahrhundert* (Freiburg and Munich, 1956), chaps. iv–x.

were expected to harmonize with each
cally but because right-minded men—n... ...
by private but by public interests—would naturally find
ways of reconciling them. Parties—defined in Walpole's
time precisely as Madison would define them over half a
century later in *The Federalist*—were the malign result of
"the gratifying of private passion by public means," and
"faction is to party," Bolingbroke wrote, "what the super-
lative is to the positive: party is a political evil, and faction is the worst of all parties."[23]

Not all formed opposition, in theory at least, was
necessarily factious. Some, motivated by public concerns,
directed not to private gain but public good, was occa-
sionally said, at least by mid-century, to be necessary for
a free state and to have a legal basis in the right of the
subject to petition the crown. And there was always the
entering wedge for a legitimate opposition in the argument that though the King could do no wrong his servants
certainly could, and were in fact betraying him, and that
therefore formed opposition was the most devoted kind

[23] "The Idea of a Patriot King," in *The Works of . . . Henry
St. John, Lord Viscount Bolingbroke* (London, 1754), III, 83.
On the problem of parties and the concept of party in the mid-
eighteenth century, the dominant view is still that of Namier
(summarized in his Romanes Lecture, cited in note 17 above,
and developed further by Richard Pares in *George III and the
Politicians,* Oxford, 1953); see in addition, Foord, "His Majesty's
Opposition, especially pp. 37ff., and Brooke, "Introductory Survey," pp. 183ff. Caroline Robbins has explored the deviant
"acceptance of party by Englishmen" in the period before 1770
in her article " 'Discordant Parties,' . . ." *Political Science
Quarterly,* 73 (1958), 505–529; the nature of the deviance
helps illuminate the normal condemnation of party and faction
and the standard advocacy of uniformity of opinion and non-
partisanship in public service.

ᴏf loyalty to the King. But this implied that the King was either impotent or witless, and in any case offered none but subjective criteria for distinguishing narrow factionalism from high-minded opposition. Objective criteria were never forthcoming, were in fact impossible to devise in the existing political and intellectual context, and the condemnation of faction and the hostility to party persisted through the period, endorsed not only by every administration seeking to condemn contestors of its power but also by opposition groups asserting the purity of their motives. Opposition, by its very nature, therefore—by the very structure of the political system—fed the fears of conspiracy, nourished the administration's belief that it existed in a state of siege and was continuously threatened by *coups d'état*.

The opposition fed these apprehensions also in a converse and more important sense. It did so by charging, and endlessly reiterating the claim, that the government itself was factious, that it was the King's ministry and not its opponents that nourished designs against the constitution and plotted the overthrow of English liberties. The fear of conspiracy was created, in other words, not only by what Walpole feared in his enemies but what his enemies said they feared in him.

It would be difficult to exaggerate the bitterness, the virulence, the savagery of the attacks on Walpole's ministry by the opposition press—and difficult also to exaggerate the importance of these attacks in the origins of American politics. For it was the opposition press, as much as any single influence, that shaped the political awareness of eighteenth-century Americans; it was the opposition version of politics, past and present, that became the ordinary presumption of informed Americans.

The voice of the opposition—shrill, persistent, penetrating—poured from the teeming public prints of the day. The newspapers, periodicals, pamphlets, even the ballads and at times the high poetry in the age of George II, carried slashing attacks on the government; slanderous, vituperative attacks, often veiled in allegory and allusion but unmistakable in intent. The greatest writers of the age—Swift, Defoe, Pope, Gay, Fielding—contributed, and there was a host of lesser contributors, ranging from highly placed, committed amateurs concerned with a few specific ideological and political issues to hack professionals capable of writing on any subject from any point of view, vigorously, shrewdly, and endlessly. In this welter of opposition publicity two series of writings, voicing the views of groups at opposite ends of the opposition spectrum—groups opposed in ultimate ideological origins but yet identical in anti-administration animus—stand out.

The first, inheritors of seventeeth-century libertarianism, stood primarily for individual rights against the power of the state, and associated themselves with the republican theorists of the Civil War period, descending from Milton and Harrington through Neville, Sidney, and Locke. These radicals of the early eighteenth century included such highly placed figures as Robert Viscount Molesworth, but they were for the most part less eminent: intransigent dissenters elaborating a system of political thought around a central theological and ecclesiastical core, and coffeehouse pamphleteers and journalists who kept alive strains of seventeenth-century political extremism that most politicians in Hanoverian England would gladly have forgotten. The most effective writers of this motley "left-wing" group—effective in England for a brief period, effective in America throughout the century—were the Old Whig pamphleteer John Trenchard, active as an extreme liberal in politics as far back as the Exclusion Crisis of 1679, and Thomas Gordon, an ambitious and phenomenally successful Scots journalist many years Trenchard's junior who collaborated with him first in *The Independent Whig* (1720), devoted largely to attacking the High Church, and then in the series of articles signed "Cato" that appeared in *The London Journal* and *The British Journal* and that were collected into a four-volume book called *Cato's Letters*. These 144 pieces originally published between November 1720 and December 1723 were "among the most troublesome thorns that pricked the vulnerable sides of the British ministry," and they were intellectually among the most important. Though they differed on certain points from the views of other radical writers, they incorporated in their colorful, slashing, superbly readable pages major themes of the opposition intelligentsia, and imprinted them indelibly on the "country" mind in both England and America.[24]

[24] Charles B. Realey, *The London Journal and Its Authors, 1720–1723* (*Bulletin of the University of Kansas*, XXXVI, no. 23, December 1, 1935), 237. On *Cato's Letters* generally, see references in Bailyn, *Ideological Origins*, pp. 35–37.

The skeleton of their political thought was Lockean —concerned with inalienable rights and the contract theory of government—but only the skeleton. The flesh, the substance, the major preoccupations and the underlying motivations and mood, were quite different, as was, of course, the level of discourse. For these coffeehouse radicals and pamphleteers the political world was a struggle between power and liberty, in which power "has almost constantly been the aggressor . . . Power is like fire; it warms, scorches, or destroys according as it is watched, provoked, or increased." And increased the fires of power most often were, for if there was one absolute certainty, one unqualified fact, it was that in his deepest nature man was "restless and selfish," ruled "not by principle, but by passion," driven by an uncontrollable lust for domination, frail and uncertain in judgment, and susceptible to manipulation by the inveterate enemies of liberty. Power, impelled by these passions of men, had desolated the earth; where liberty was extinguished so too in the end were justice, virtue, honesty, trade, naval power, wealth, even a high birth rate—indeed, everything worth living for: the arts and sciences, thought, understanding, religion. Printing, it was noted, had vanished in that most perfect of all tyrannies, Turkey; and in Asia, "formerly full of people, you are now forced to travel by the compass: there are no roads, houses, nor inhabitants. The sun is left to scorch up the grass and fruits which it has raised, or the rain to rot them."

Who that has human compassion can help feeling the sorrows of his wretched race and behold unconcerned the forlorn and abject state of mankind? Monks deceiving, alarming, and spunging them; their governors taxing, mulcting, and squeezing them; soldiers harassing, oppressing, and butchering them! . . . Nor do things mend; on the contrary, the mischiefs and misfortunes of the world grow hourly greater, and its inhabitants thinner.

Everywhere, in the absolute monarchies that covered most of the earth, there was "ignorance, vice, poverty, and vileness." Thus had "despotic power . . . defaced the creation and laid the world waste"—"in all countries," that is, "except our own, and a very few more." For, they wrote, "we have a constitution that abhors absolute power; we have a king that does not desire it; and we are a people that will never suffer it." To be sure, a commonwealth, that is, a republic, was ideally the most perfect government for the attainment of liberty, but a perfect commonwealth would require a perfectly equal distribution of property, these neo-Harringtonians said, to attain which would cost incalculable bloodshed and upheaval; as it was, "our government is a thousand degrees nearer akin to a commonwealth . . . than it is to absolute monarchy," and the result was certainly excellent. "No nation in the world enjoys the *liberty* which *England* enjoys," they wrote; its uniquely successful mixture of government should be left undisturbed and protected. For liberty, they agreed, had been preserved by the "control and counterpoise" of the several parts of the constitution; if that balance failed, particularly if "the interest of the magistracy" invaded that of the other elements of the constitution, the people would no longer be able "to keep power from oppression, and their magistrates from changing into plunderers and murderers." The danger of that happening, they wrote, was perpetual. If the vigilance of the people was ever thoroughly softened by negligence, sloth, or corruption, the ever-watchful monopolists of power would soon act. Long before, in his immensely popular and influential tracts against standing armies, Trenchard had warned of these dangers, and in the early 1720's he and Gordon elaborated the warning:

> Public corruptions and abuses have grown upon us; fees in most, if not in all, offices, are immensely increased; places and employments, which ought not to be sold at all, are sold for treble values; the necessities of the public have made greater impositions unavoidable, and yet the public has run very much in debt; and as those debts have been increasing, and the people growing poor, salaries have been augmented, and pensions multiplied.

It was in just such times of ripe corruption that ministerial vultures characteristically lunged for illegal power, building up to their final *coups* by well-known techniques: the impoverishment of the people by costly wars, the preferment to office of "worthless and wicked men," the promotion of "luxury, idleness, and expense, and a general depravation of manners," and ultimately the deliberate provocation of "the people to disaffection" in order to create "an argument for new oppression." Thus it had always been in all countries; but in free states, where the people have a voice in government, the threats took on a special form.

> They will endeavor to bribe the electors in the choice of their representatives and so to get a council of their own creatures; and where they cannot succeed with the electors, they will endeavor to corrupt the deputies after they are chosen . . . and to draw into the perpetration of their crimes those very men from whom the betrayed people expect the redress of their grievances and the punishment of those crimes.[25]

Such were the "measures . . . actually taken by wicked and desperate ministers to ruin and enslave their country." To this great and immediate danger—this glaring danger, it seemed to the radical opposition in the age of Walpole—and to the underlying problem of corruption, Trenchard and Gordon devoted some of their most vivid pages. In prose that would long be considered a model of invective, they renewed "the crackling Whiggism of 1679," but with the conspirators against the community no longer Jesuit assailants of the government but the government itself.[26] In this they were by no means alone. The associated dangers of ministerial

[25] The quotations in the paragraph above are from *Cato's Letters,* nos. 25, 40, 44, 48, 37, 32, 70, 20, 17 (in the four-volume collection, 5th ed., London, 1748: I, 191, 192; II, 50, 77; I, 186; II, 108; I, 191; II, 107, 28; I, 254; III, 14; I, 140–141, 114, 115–116). But the same points are elaborated throughout the *Letters*; note particularly nos. 33, 43, 47, 73, and 85.
[26] *Ibid.,* I, 111; John Carswell, *The South Sea Bubble* (London, 1960), p. 247.

usurpation and social and political corruption were the central concerns of the profuse opposition literature of the time—that "steady stream of political writing" that elaborated the central themes of the anti-court opposition.[27] If "Cato" was the most famous and influential Cassandra of the "left" segment of the opposition, *The Craftsman* was the great denunciator of the "right."

The Craftsman was largely written by and remained throughout its spectacular existence the mouthpiece of the brilliant, cultivated, unscrupulous Jacobite politician, writer, and philosopher, Henry St. John, Viscount Bolingbroke. It appeared weekly or semi-weekly for a full ten years, from 1726 to 1736, and, republished in book form, it fills thirteen volumes. Its savage, bitter, relentless attacks on Walpole, merging on fundamental points with those of Cato—indeed, *The Craftsman* quotes the writings of Trenchard and other libertarians wholesale—constituted "the first example in British political history of an effective long-term propaganda campaign."[28] Its claims, however cynically conceived, however extravagant and politically calculating, exploited the major political concerns of the age, and none more so than the fear of corruption—corruption generally, in the sense of moral and social dissoluteness, and corruption technically, in the sense of the deliberate manipulation of elections and of voting in the House of Commons to create

[27] Foord, *His Majesty's Opposition,* p. 168. "Opposition writers hammered away for seventeen years with deadly and often hysterical insistence upon the same points: the unconstitutional position, corrupt methods, and vicious policies of the Minister" (p. 170).

[28] *Ibid.,* p. 170.

a ministerial preponderance. "Robinocracy"[29]—the monopoly of power by Robert Walpole as "prime" minister (a term introduced now in derogation)—was the major theme, an obsessive theme, that runs through the 495 issues of *The Craftsman*.

It was a natural enough phenomenon, Bolingbroke explained. Public ministers naturally "lie under great temptations, through the infirmities and corruption of human nature, to prefer their own *private interest* to that of the *community* . . . *wicked ministers* have exerted their endeavors, in all ages, to abridge the liberties of the people and wrest the laws to the punishment of their fellow-subjects." But the immediate form of ministerial corruption in England under Walpole was unique. "Robinocracy," Bolingbroke explained, was a form of government seemingly

> compounded of a *monarchy,* an *aristocracy,* and a *democracy,* for it consists in keeping all *three* in a state of dependency upon itself. The *Robinarch,* or chief ruler, is nominally a *minister* only and creature of the prince; but in reality he is a *sovereign,* as despotic, arbitrary a sovereign as this part of the world affords . . . The *Robinarch* . . . hath unjustly engrossed the whole power of a nation into his own hands . . . [and] admits no person to any considerable post of trust and power under him who is not either a *relation,* a *creature,* or a *thorough-paced tool* whom he can lead at pleasure

[29] The plays on Robert Walpole's name by the opposition satirists were endless: "Gay's *Beggar's Opera* (1728) satirised 'Robin of Bagshot [the haunt of highwaymen], alias Gorgon, alias Bluff Bob, alias Carbuncle, alias Bob Booty.'" A. R. Humphreys, *The Augustan World* (London, 1954), p. 111.

into any dirty work without being able to discover his designs or the consequences of them.

Since in England the ministry must operate within a mixed constitution where deputies of the people share in government, it therefore becomes necessary for one who seeks *"Robinarchal power"*

> to secure the *deputies* of the people on his side, as well as the *Prince* himself . . . Some are tied down with *honors, titles,* and *preferments,* of which the *Robinarch* engrosses the disposal to himself, and others with *bribes,* which are called *pensions* in these countries. Some are persuaded to prostitute themselves for the lean reward of *hopes* and *promises*; and others, more senseless than all of them, have sacrificed their principles and consciences to a set of *party names* without any meaning, or the vanity of appearing in favor at *court.*

Once in power the Robinarchal ministry, "this new-fangled medley of government," feeds on its own corruption; it loads the people with taxes and with debts and ends by creating a mercenary army ostensibly for the purpose of protecting the people but in fact to perfect its dominance in just those ways, Bolingbroke said, that Trenchard had explained years before in his tracts on standing armies.

Yet the catastrophic cycle, spun from corruption and impelled by ministerial designs, could be broken. If the cries of the people became loud and importunate enough, Bolingbroke wrote, they would eventually penetrate the cloud of deliberate falsehoods and malicious distortions by which power-hungry ministers misrepresented the aims and feelings of the people to the Prince in order to keep him pliant and satisfied. Once the truth pierced this contrived shell of misinformation, the Prince, Bolingbroke explained, "makes enquiry into their complaints, and finding them just, rouses himself up to vengeance, and resolves to redress them." Thus that romantic ideal, the Patriot Prince, who should govern as well as reign, yet govern above parties and factions "in harmony with a loyal and independent Commons."[30]

These were extreme voices of the opposition. On major points of doctrine their views were not different from those generally expressed in Georgian England; the difference lay in the emphasis. Writers in the mainstream and in the opposition counter-current wrote from the same basic set of beliefs, but where the one group stressed the benefits of the balance of England's mixed constitution, the other pointed to the difficulties of maintaining it in the face of ministerial encroachments. Where the standard stress was on the history of English liberty and the tradition of political integrity, the opposition pointed to the sudden appearance of what they believed to be the systematic effort of "The Robinarch" to corrupt the electorate, and the uncontrollable machinations of a newly-risen money interest, unknown to the constitution, that battened on the poor and helpless and bought favors

[30] *The Craftsman* (collected ed., London, 1731–37), VI, 111; V, 152–153, 155, 156; H. N. Fieldhouse, "Bolingbroke and the Idea of Non-Party Government," *History*, n.s., 23 (1938–39), 53.

wholesale of the government.[31] Where the common pane-
gyrics of the age sang the praises of England's historically
benevolent environment, an environment that had bred
and sustained liberty so successfully in the past, opposition
writers pointed ahead to the likely consequences of London's squalor and of the rising incidence of dissoluteness
in a society gone wild with the meretricious pleasures of
affluence. Four parts out of five of Thomson's *Liberty*
explore the failures of other nations to preserve liberty, and
celebrate that goddess' re-establishment, after centuries of
flight, on Albion's blessed shore, "where, King and people
equal bound / By guardian laws, [her] fullest blessings
flow." But the poem is dedicated to Frederick, Prince of
Wales, the notorious patron of the opposition, and Part V,
"The Prospect," is a diatribe on "corruption's soul-deject-

[31] The fear of a rising "money interest" drawing wealth and
power from esoteric sources independent of the land and its
people and creating not only enervating luxury and corruption
generally but, specifically, dangers to the constitution in the
resources it could make available to ambitious ministries, was
a powerful element in eighteenth-century opposition thought.
Its expressions are manifold—as voluminous in *Cato's Letters*
(the first ten numbers are almost entirely devoted to the catastrophic example of the South Sea Company) as in *The Craftsman* and the writings of less committed spokesmen of the
landed interest. For Bolingbroke's fear of the influence of "the
bank, the East India Company, and in general the moneyed
interest," and his association of "the trade of Parliament and
the trade of funds," see references in Jeffery Hart, *Viscount
Bolingbroke* (London, 1965), p. 30. For a particularly vivid
expression of this fear as it entered into the American Revolutionary controversy, see the elder Pitt's explanation of the
reason why "the constitution at this moment stands violated,"
namely, the "influx of wealth into this country . . . [that is
not] the regular, natural produce of labor and industry" b͎ͅ t
merely "the riches of Asia" which "have brought with ͭ͑
not only Asiatic luxury but, I fear, Asiatic principles ͬ
ernment," quoted in Bailyn, *Ideological Origins*, pp. ͅ

ing arts" and an empurpled plea to the British people to preserve, against all the evils of the time, the three virtues which alone would sustain the nation's freedom: "independent life; / Integrity in office; and o'er all / Supreme, a passion for the commonweal." The poem, for all its celebration of England's glory, makes explicit what had been only implicit in Thomson's writing, before and would culminate in *Edward and Eleonora* (1739), banned by the Licensing Act of 1737: the claim that England was sunk in enervating luxury, the paradoxical result of England's success in commerce and the source of irreversibly degenerative corruption. What began as an elaborate panegyric ended as an opposition tract. "The general course of politics in 1736 and 1737," the poem's modern analyst concludes, "seems to have accentuated the Opposition sentiments that could be read into *Liberty*, and even to some extent to have altered the application of the poem." Increasingly politics had that effect, with the result, Professor Robbins writes, that by mid-century "complacency in England herself was sharply declining. The 'Forty-five seemed to many to have revealed shocking decadence and weakness in the face of undisciplined and not very numerous invaders. The confusions that ensued after Walpole's fall . . . were disillusioning . . . In the fifties renewed war, unexpected dangers, earthquakes, and defeats threw the country into a fury of excitement over the militia once again and over the 'times.' Disunion, faction, luxury, vice, a loss of old courage and devotion to liberty, these afforded the moralist texts for many a sermon and tract." And the text multiplied. Henry

Fielding, who had blasted the rapaciousness and corruption of Walpole's administration in *The Champion* (1739–42), turned in *The True Patriot* (1745–46) to a general denunciation of the "monstrous impieties and iniquities" that abounded "in what is called the World" in an effort to recall a dispirited, demoralized, and fearful people to greatness. James Burgh's *Britain's Remembrancer* (1746) is a violent denunciation of "our degenerate times and corrupt nation" and a passionate warning of the "legion of furies" descending on England: "venality, perjury, faction, opposition to legal authority, idleness, gluttony, drunkenness, lewdness, excessive gaming, robberies, clandestine marriages, breach of matrimonial vows, self-murders"; and though its author was a nonconformist radical of deepest dye, his pamphlet became current in more than sectarian circles. A decade later John Brown's blackly despondent lament, *An Estimate of the Manners and Principles of the Times* (1757), became famous throughout the realm.[32]

[32] *Liberty,* Part I, lines 317, 318; Part V, lines 307, 120; McKillop, "Background of Thomson's *Liberty*," pp. 94, 95; Caroline Robbins, *The Eighteenth-Century Commonwealthman* (Cambridge, 1959), pp. 277, 278–279; [Fielding], *The True Patriot: and The History of Our Own Times* (Miriam A. Locke, ed., [University] Alabama, 1964), facing p. 80; [Burgh], *Britain's Remembrancer: or the Danger Not Over. Being . . . A Brief View, from History, of the Effects of the Vices Which Now Prevail in Britain, Upon the Greatest Empires and States of Former Times . . .* (London, 1746), p. 6. The evolution of Thomson's politics is reflected significantly in his writing. His *Poem on the Death of Sir Isaac Newton* (1727) was dedicated to Walpole. *Britannia*, written in the same year, is in part a polemic against the British government's pusillanimity in the face of Spanish insults; but it also praises peace (and hence Walpole), and in any case was withheld from publication for

The dominant mood was still optimistic, still proud, confident, and complacent. But the undercurrents of apprehension, powerfully stirred by an indefatigable opposition, ran deep and strong.

Of this was the political culture of early eighteenth-century England composed: a conviction of national superiority manifested particularly in the achievement of a degree of civil and political freedom unique in the world; the belief that this freedom resulted from the careful

---

two years, and then appeared only anonymously, "the apparent reason for this caution being that he was trying his luck with Walpole." The passages of *The Seasons* written in 1730 (*Autumn* and the revision of *Winter*) warn "at great length against the corrosive effects of luxury and corruption, though there is still hope for the British, Liberty's chosen people." *Sophonisba* (the heroine is in effect a female Cato), also published in 1730, was dedicated to the Queen, Thomson's affinity with the opposition at that point still being "not a firm bond, but a slant or bias." And while *Liberty*, written five years later, only at the end turns into an opposition diatribe, by 1737 a group of Thomson's casual verses indicate "his open adherence to the Opposition" (he was by then a pensionary of Prince Frederick), and the banned *Edward and Eleonora*, dedicated to the Princess, forthrightly includes the character of a wicked minister as "the symbol of a vaguely defined evil called Ministerial Power . . . [who] is obviously Walpole, just as the king whom he misleads is obviously George II." McKillop, "Background of Thomson's *Liberty*," pp. 7, 89, 91; Mable H. Cable, "The Idea of a Patriot King in the Propaganda of the Opposition to Walpole, 1735–1739," *Philological Quarterly* 18 (1939), 124n, 125. See also McKillop, "Ethics and Political History in Thomsons' *Liberty*" and Louis I. Bredvold, "The Gloom of the Tory Satirists," in James L. Clifford and Louis A. Landa, eds., *Pope and His Contemporaries* (Oxford, 1949). On Bolingbroke's confirmed pessimism over England's prospects, which is the conceptual starting point of his *Idea of a Patriot King* (1738), see Hart, *Bolingbroke*, pp. 93, 97, and chaps. v and vi generally.

balancing of the socio-constitutional elements in a mixed government; and the experience of politics itself as the exercise of an elaborate system of "influence" by which the crown and its administration controlled the whole of the polity—a control, informal and un-legal, that was condemned as corrupt by vituperative and indefatigable critics of the government, themselves viewed as quasi-conspirators against constituted power.

Much of the opposition theorizing was cynical, pure "grumbletonianism" by the outs against the ins; and often what started out as a sincere expression of the universal and realistic fear of an over-great government ended on dizzying heights of rhetoric where the aspects of reality could no longer be perceived. Yet if the opposition literature of early eighteenth-century politics was often hyperbolic and rhetorical, magnifying beliefs and exaggerating fears, the beliefs and fears were nevertheless there, not as neurotic fantasies but as realistic responses to the recent history and existing condition of public life in England. And they are essential to our story. For these ideas, these beliefs, fears and perceptions, became primary elements of American politics in its original, early eighteenth-century form: primary in the sense of forming assumptions and expectations, of furnishing not merely the vocabulary but the grammar of thought, the apparatus by which the world was perceived.

The veneration of the British constitution, defined as mixed government precisely as it was in England, was a commonplace in America from the earliest years of the eighteenth century. Nor does this require particular explanation, for communication was continuous between England and the colonies, and the English government was as much a concern of Americans as it was of Englishmen. More remarkable is the speed with which the colonists soaked up the protest literature of the opposition and incorporated its main propositions into their basic perceptions of public life.[33] Individual issues of *Cato's Letters* were reprinted again and again, referred to and quoted in every possible context, in every colony in America. James Franklin began reprinting the *Letters* in his *New England Courant* eleven months after the first of them appeared in London; Zenger's *New York Weekly Journal* in the 1730's was a veritable anthology of these extraordinarily popular essays, as were the *South Carolina Gazette* and Boston's *Independent Advertiser* in the forties and the *Pennsylvania Journal* in the fiftes. So influential was *Cato's Letters* in the colonies, so packed with ideological meaning, that, reinforced by Addison's universally popular play *Cato* and the colonists' selectively Whiggish reading of the Roman historians, it gave rise to what might be called a "Catonic" image, personifying the whole of opposition thought, in which the career of the half-mythological Roman and the words of the two London journalists merged indistinguishably. Everyone who read the *Boston Gazette* of April 26, 1756, understood the double reference—bibliographical and historical—that was intended by an anonymous writer who concluded an

[33] For documentation of the statements in this and the following two paragraphs, see Bailyn, *Ideological Origins*, pp. 43ff., and Anna J. DeArmond, *Andrew Bradford, Colonial Journalist* (Newark, Del., 1949), pp. 166ff.

address to the people of Massachusetts, as he put it without further explanation, "in the words of Cato to the freeholders of Great Britain."

Trenchard and Gordon's *Independent Whig* was no less influential. When William Livingston and others of the so-called "Presbyterian" group in New York wished to found a journal in opposition to the government in 1752, they deliberately modeled their periodical, *The Independent Reflector,* on *The Independent Whig.* Isaac Norris, in Pennsylvania, ordered his bookseller in 1721 to send him the separate issues of *The Independent Whig* as soon as they appeared in London, and that whole collection was reprinted in its entirety in Philadelphia in 1740. Bolingbroke's *Craftsman* too was drawn on repeatedly, paraphrased, quoted, cribbed—cited in some of the least likely circumstances as "the most masterly performance that ever was wrote upon the *British* constitution"[34]—as were other leading voices of the opposition press, and a wide range of other writers who argued the same points with less evident political animus. So Burgh's *Remembrancer* was reprinted entire in the colonies three times before 1760, and Brown's *An Estimate* at least once. The key writers throughout, however, remained the venerable Trenchard, with his roots in the controversies of the reign of Charles II, and his collaborator Gordon, "that solid and inimitable writer," as he was referred to in

---

[34] *The Maryland Gazette Extraordinary; An Appendix to No. 162,* June 4, 1748, p. [3], where Bolingbroke's *Dissertation on Parties* is quoted as a gloss on Locke's contract theory of government.

New York in 1755,[35] who elaborated his earlier writings in his popular and influential translations of Sallust and Tacitus, which, prefaced by interpretative discourses hundreds of pages long, were in fact "country" tracts as flamboyant as his periodical pieces.

The real question, however, is not what was available in print in the colonies but what the available publications meant to their readers. And on this the evidence is profuse and unmistakable. The opposition vision of English politics, conveyed through these popular opposition writers, was determinative of the political understanding of eighteenth-century Americans. The colonists universally agreed that man was by nature lustful, that he was utterly untrustworthy in power, unable to control his passion for domination. The antinomy of power and liberty was accepted as the central fact of politics, and with it the belief that power was aggressive, liberty passive, and that the duty of free men was to protect the latter and constrain the former. Threats to free government, it was believed, lurked everywhere, but nowhere more dangerously than in the designs of ministers in office to aggrandize power by the corrupt use of influence, and by this means ultimately to destroy the balance of the constitution. Corruption, especially in the form of the manipulation and the bribery of the Commons by the gift of places, pensions, and sinecures, was as universal a cry in the colonies as it was in England, and with it the same sense of despair at the state of the rest of the world, the

[35] "The Watch-Tower, No. XV," *New York Mercury*, March 3, 1755.

same belief that tyranny, already dominant over most of the earth, was continuing to spread its menace and was threatening even that greatest bastion of liberty, England itself.

The political culture of colonial America—the assumptions, expectations, patterns of responses, and clusters of information relevant to the conduct of public affairs—was thus British, but British with a peculiar emphasis. It was not simply a miscellaneous amalgam of ideas and beliefs current in eighteenth-century England, nor, most emphatically, was it simply a distillation of the thought of a few great minds, particularly Locke's. It was, rather, a pattern of ideas, assumptions, attitudes, and beliefs given distinctive shape by the opposition elements in English politics, those elements whose attack on "influence" and ministerial corruption was "the one idealistic feature of early eighteenth-century [English] politics, the only political programme which could appeal to men with a sense of moral purpose."[36] It was primarily this opposition frame of mind through which the colonists saw the world and in terms of which they themselves became participants in politics.

That this should have been the case was in part the result of the sheer availability and attractiveness of the opposition literature. But in greater part it was the result of the peculiar persuasiveness of these ideas in the

[36] J. H. Plumb, *England in the Eighteenth Century* (Harmondsworth, England, 1950), p. 105.

57

context of American politics. For political life in America, while similar to England's in important respects, was yet significantly different in ways that would give a heightened meaning and a sharper relevance to—would make more obvious, more vital, and more necessary—the libertarian doctrines of coffeehouse radicals and the rancor of the anti-"Robinarchs."

II

THE STRUCTURE OF
COLONIAL POLITICS

A‍T PRESENT," wrote Dr. William Douglass of Boston in his *Summary, Historical and Political . . . of the British Settlements in North America* (1749–51), the governments of the colonies of British North America

> in conformity to our legislature in Great Britain . . . consist of three separate negatives; thus, by the governor, representing the King, the colonies are monarchical; by the Council, they are aristocratical; by a house of representatives or delegates from the people, they are democratical: these three are distinct and independent of one another, and the colonies enjoy the conveniences of each of these forms of government without their inconveniences, the several negatives being checks upon one another. The concurrence of these three forms of government seems to be the highest perfection that human civil government can attain to in times of peace . . . ; if it did not sound too profane by making too free with the mystical expressions of our religion, I should call it *a trinity in unity*.

Douglass had reason to be concerned about his reputation for profanity. Long before, in the great controversy over smallpox inoculation, he was said to have been an anticlerical heretic who violated the Sixth Commandment and deserved to be stuck in the pillory; his comparison of the colonial governments to the Trinity was promptly condemned as a blasphemous libel, a proper expression of "the most complete and undisguised system of atheism that . . . was ever dared to be published in a *Christian* country." But if his religious views were heretical his constitutional theories were orthodox. His belief that the colonial governments at mid-century "in conformity to our legislature in Great Britain" were replicas, however imperfect, of England's famous mixed and balanced constitution was altogether representative of the thinking of the time.[1]

Belief in a fundamental correspondence between the English constitution and the separate colonial constitutions, almost an axiom of political thought in eighteenth-century America, had gained currency rapidly at the end of the seventeenth century. It had emerged from the conjunction of two quite independent developments: on the one hand, the appearance almost everywhere in the colonies of bicameral legislative bodies—a response not

---

[1] Douglass, *Summary*, I, 213–214. Douglass' book first appeared as a series of pamphlets, the fourteenth of which contained the quoted passage, and was attacked in *The Boston Weekly News Letter*, June 10 and June 16, 1748. Douglass replied on July 11 in *The Independent Advertiser*, explaining that the controversial phrase had been written "in a poetical strain, in an *Asiatic* florid *idiom*"—a "rapture"—by which to express his veneration for the British constitution.

to constitutional theories but to immediate needs and problems; and on the other hand, the acceptance generally in England, and the public discussion there, of the concept of mixed government in the terms laid down by Charles I in his classic *Answer to the XIX. Propositions of Both Houses of Parliament* (1642). By the early eighteenth century English constitutional theory was commonly applied to American institutions as the lower houses of the colonial legislatures came more definitely to stand for local, popular interests and the upper houses, the colonial Councils, appeared to approximate the classical upper chambers, prototypically the House of Lords. It was by then generally felt that the colonial legislatures were, as one governor put it, "umbras of an English parliament."[2]

Crown and proprietary officials, to be sure, frequently scoffed at the idea that these local institutions were analogous to England's Parliament. But even they were led, willy-nilly, by the sheer magnetism of the English model, to help recreate the system of mixed government in America; they were obliged by force of political circumstance to act as if the model fitted.[3] In the colonies

[2] Governor Thomas Lynch of Jamaica, 1683, quoted in Leonard W. Labaree, *Royal Government in America* (New Haven, 1930), p. 214.

[3] So Governor Burnet told the Massachusetts House in 1728 that the British Parliaments "have a just claim to be a pattern to the Assemblies in the plantations . . . The three distinct branches of the legislature, preserved in due balance, form the excellency of the *British* constitution: if any one of these branches should become less able to support its own dignity and freedom, the whole must inevitably suffer by the alteration. I need not draw the parallel at length; it speaks for itself."

the informed population at large, habituated to think in terms of correspondences, their minds controlled by what E. M. W. Tillyard has called a "passion for concatenation," knew with intuitive certainty that, despite the technical difficulties that stood in the way of such a belief, the public world that enclosed them was built of corresponding constitutions, one local and palpable, the other metropolitan and transcendent, equivalent in function and form. Such irregularities and exceptions as there were, they believed with Douglass, "doubtless in time will be rectified."[4]

And why should they have doubted that time would continue to narrow the differences between the two constitutions? So much of the distance had already been covered. By the early eighteenth century the confusion and institutional crudities of the settlement period had long since been overcome. Institutions originally created

---

Journals of the House of Representatives of Massachusetts, 1727–1729 (Boston, 1927), pp. 245–246. Similarly, Lord Baltimore in 1733 recommended to the Lower House in Maryland "a Parliamentary proceeding in your method of doing business, nor can you copy better than after our mother country." Charles A. Barker, *The Background of the Revolution in Maryland* (New Haven, 1940), p. 155. The development of the lower house in Maryland is particularly illuminating; see Barker, *Background in Maryland,* chap. v, and, generally, Mary P. Clarke, *Parliamentary Privilege in the American Colonies* (New Haven, 1943).

[4] W. H. Greenleaf, *Order, Empiricism and Politics . . . 1500– 1700* (London, 1964), p. 21, where Tillyard's phrase introduces a discussion of " 'argument by correspondence,' a . . . process of reasoning [that] consisted in reviewing, often at very great length, the similarity between things, in taking a known fact or situation in one plane of being and inferring that a corresponding fact or situation existed in another plane." Douglass' remark is in *Summary,* I, 215.

to control private organizations had evolved into organs of public government. In all the colonies—royal, corporate, and proprietary—there were single executives (in the royal governments the executives were explicitly denominated the King's vicegerents). Every colony had its representative assembly whose members, like the members of the House of Commons in England, presumably spoke for "the democracy" and were chosen for the most part by electors qualified by the same forty-shilling freehold that predominated in England. And every colony had its upper chamber which, however irregularly constituted by European standards, could be said in some measure to stand between the polar forces of power and liberty.

The analogy was compelling; ran deeper than thought; shaped the very process of thought; and remained therefore resistant to the incongruent political details that appeared daily in all the colonies. Indeed, the political incongruities increased in number and importance at the same time as the formal organs of the government appeared to grow in their likeness to England's. By mid-century it was clear that if the formal organs of government and the constitutional structure of the colonial communities were strikingly similar to England's, something fundamental in their operation was very different. For while in England the mixed and balanced constitution appeared to produce a high degree of public harmony and the peaceful integration of political forces, similar institutions in the colonies produced the opposite. There was bitter, persistent strife within the provincial governments almost everywhere. There was strife, first of all, between branches of government—between the executives on the one hand and the legislatures on the other —strife so rampant as to be more noteworthy by its absence than its presence and so intense as to lead on occasions to a total paralysis of government. But it was not only a matter of conflict between branches of government. There was, besides this, a milling factionalism that transcended institutional boundaries and at times reduced the politics of certain colonies to an almost unchartable chaos of competing groups. Some were personal groups, small clusters of relatives and friends that rose suddenly at particular junctures and faded again as quickly, merging into other equally unstable configurations. Others were economic, regional, and more generally social interest groups, some quickly rising and more quickly falling, some durable, persisting through a generation or more, though never highly organized and consequently only irregularly active and prominent and continuously shifting in personnel. Still others (though these were fewer) were groups formed to defend and advance programs that transcended immediate personal or group interests. All were vocal; most were difficult to control; and while in certain colonies at certain times political life attained the hoped-for balance and tranquillity, there was scarcely a governor in the eighteenth century who at one time or another did not echo the weary question and the anguished admonition of William Penn to the political leaders of the City of Brotherly Love a mere four years after it was founded: "Cannot more friendly and private courses be taken to set matters right in an infant province? . . . For the love of God, me, and the poor country, be not so *governmentish!*"[5]

But Pennsylvania remained, in Penn's words, "noisy and open in [its] dissatisfactions" through all the ninety-five years of its colonial history. There, as elsewhere, conflict seemed to rise irresistibly from deep-lying sources. How profound the disorder, how fundamental the malaise, is perhaps best indicated by the speed with which humble, crude disputes—disputes of the crassest, least principled character—skidded off their original tracks onto elevating planes of disputation and ended deadlocked in the realm of principle. The surface of public life at the level of provincial government was thin and easily broken through. So the Zenger affair, which ended in a world-famous controversy over basic principles of freedom of the press, began over a newly appointed governor's demand for a fifty per cent cut of the income collected in office by his temporary predecessor.[6]

What was the cause of the malaise within the colonial governments? Why was the surface of public life so brittle? Many explanations have been given of one or another conflict or group of conflicts. But if one takes the colonies all in all something more general seems to be called for, some means of arriving at elements common to all the colonies and all the varieties of controversies. A compari-

[5] Samuel M. Janney, *The Life of William Penn . . . ,* 2nd ed. (Philadelphia, 1852), pp. 277–278.

[6] On the politics of the Zenger affair, see Stanley N. Katz's Introduction to James Alexander's *Brief Narrative of the Case and Trial of John Peter Zenger* (Cambridge, 1963); for a particularly good example of the fragility of colonial politics, see M. Eugene Sirmans, *Colonial South Carolina, A Political History, 1663–1763* (Chapel Hill, 1966), pp. 282ff., 301ff.

son would seem useful, not of one colony with another or one conflict with another, by way of arriving at common elements, but of the whole of colonial politics in its structural aspects with what is relevant in the experience of eighteenth-century England. For if contemporaries were struck by the similarities between the formal structure of government in England and in America, historians have reason to be struck by the differences in the informal structure of politics.

The similarities in government were superficial; the differences in politics profound. Two mutually reinforcing sets of circumstances, the one strictly speaking political, the other more generally social or socio-political, formed the background of the controversies of the time, and these circumstances stand in contrast to the analogous conditions in England.

The first group of circumstances is quite evident and palpable in the records; it was evident and palpable at the time, and discussed at the time, but only in bits and pieces, with little sense of relationships and overall meaning. These conditions relate to what the eighteenth century called the role of power in government and what we, who conceive of the whole of government as power, describe as the role of the executive.

On the one hand, *legally,* executive power in all but two charter colonies of Rhode Island and Connecticut was far stronger in the colonies than it was in England. Three areas of power are crucial.

1) The governors in the royal and proprietary colonies had authority to exercise a veto over colonial legislation, which, further, was susceptible to disallowance by the Privy Council or the proprietors in England. The governors and the Privy Council used this power, which no English monarch exercised over the Houses of Parliament after 1707, frequently and on the most sensitive issues. Moreover, simultaneously with growth in the apparent correspondence between the colonial Assemblies and the House of Commons, the use of the executive veto was increased in two ways. First, orders were sent from England spelling out to the governors an increasing number of mandatory vetoes over whole categories of legislation, legislation declared in advance, without reference to the reasoning of the colonial Assemblies, to be inadmissible. Second, "suspending clauses," preventing enforcement of prohibited legislation until explicitly approved in England, were increasingly required. This not only strengthened the governors' hands in opposing actions of the lower houses but in effect drew the crown itself directly rather than indirectly into the business of executive negation.

2) The area of prerogative power that had been severely reduced in England in the settlement after the Glorious Revolution by the Triennial Act and that remained limited under the Septennial Act was reproduced in many of the colonies in all its archaic force. The royal governors, with very few exceptions, had the authority to prorogue and dissolve the lower houses of the Assembly, and they were accustomed to use these powers freely. In

most of the royal colonies there was no minimum frequency for convoking difficult Assemblies and no maximum duration for retaining pliant ones. Commonly, therefore, the colonial Assemblies lacked the self-determination of the House of Commons; commonly they were as dependent on executive will for their existences as the Commons had been under the Tudor and Stuart monarchs.[7]

3) The executive in the colonies had power over the judiciary explicitly denied the crown in England. The English Act of Settlement of 1701 creating permanent tenure for crown-appointed judges in England was declared to be inoperative in the colonies, and judges at all levels, from justices of the peace to chief justices of the supreme courts, were not only appointed on nomination of the governors but were dismissible by the governors' fiat. Similarly, the executive in all but the charter governments could create courts without statutory empowerment, and while it was true that both governors and the

[7] Labaree, *Royal Government,* pp. 190, 207. New Hampshire and South Carolina, among the royal colonies, had triennial acts; New York adopted a septennial act in 1743. *Ibid.,* p. 212. It is true of course that the Whig government's Septennial Act of 1716 was forced through Parliament not to restrict but to enlarge the ministry's control of the House of Commons and that repeal of the measure and "a renewed demand for annual or more frequent elections . . . became a part of the Tory, country, and radical programme, a stock-in-trade of opposition from Bolingbroke to the Chartists." But Parliaments of seven years' duration favored the ministry only because the standard, since the passage of the Triennial Act of 1693, had been Parliaments of three years' length. Walpole himself favored "a return to Parliaments without any time-limit at all." J. H. Plumb, *The Growth of Political Stability in England, 1675–1725* (London, 1967), pp. 174, 177. Cf. J. R. Pole, *Political Representation in England and the Origins of the American Republic* (London, 1966), pp. 408–412.

home government accepted tribunals created by legislative action, they never gave up their authority over the creation of courts in point of law, and exercised it repeatedly in the specific case of chancery courts. These prerogative tribunals, which sat without juries and were concerned with such unpopular matters as collecting arrears of quit rents, were creations of the governors by virtue of their chancellorship powers, and they were particularly obnoxious to the colonists. Associated with them in the colonists' minds were the vice-admiralty courts, which operated over maritime matters without juries, on civil- not common-law rules, with a scope of jurisdiction broader than that allowed the equivalent courts in England. The vice-admiralty courts too were creations not of the legislative but of the prerogative authority.[8]

In addition to these three major powers there was a variety of lesser powers also accorded the executive in America that had been eliminated in England—power over the election of the speakers of the House; power over church appointments; power over fees. But it was in these three areas primarily—the vetoing of colonial legislation; proroguing and dissolving legislative bodies; and dismissing judges and creating courts—that the legal power of the executive was felt to be most archaic and threatening, a source of danger to liberty and to the free constitution. Official explanations were offered for these

[8] For a summary of the history of executive control over the judiciary in the provincial period, see Bernard Bailyn, *Pamphlets of the American Revolution* (Cambridge, 1965–), I, 249–251; on the vice-admiralty courts, see Carl Ubbelohde, *The Vice-Admiralty Courts and the American Revolution* (Chapel Hill, 1960).

anomalies in the re-creation of England's mixed government in America (it was argued, for example, that life
tenure for judges was a poor policy where trained lawyers
were scarce but presumably increasing in number) and
exceptions were made on certain points. But neither explanation nor exception materially reduced the impact of
these anomalies on minds committed to the idea of correspondence between the greater and the lesser constitutions.

Such archaic and, to eighteenth-century Britons, self-
evidently arbitrary and threatening executive powers were
in themselves important sources of political controversy,
for they tended to mobilize the forces associated with the
legislature against those associated with the executive.
But what assured the actual conflict of these forces and
distinguished the colonial from the English constitutions
even more than the apparent exaggeration of executive
authority was the fact that an array of other circumstances
existed that radically reduced—in some places at certain
times altogether eliminated—the force of that so-called
"influence" by which the executive in England disciplined
dissent and conflict in the political community and maintained its supremacy in Parliament. The "private" constitution so crucial in making workable England's "public"
constitution of mixed government was absent in the colonies, or reduced close to the point of ineffectiveness. The
paradoxical result was that while in important respects the
colonial constitutions were archaic by eighteenth-century
standards, in other respects they were radically reformed.
The reduction of influence, of "corruption," that was so

avidly sought by a succession of would-be reformers of the
English constitution for a century after Walpole's time,
had been achieved in the mainland colonies of North
America at the beginning, almost insensibly, largely by
the force of circumstance. The original characteristics of
American politics were formed in the tensions of this
paradox.

The political influence of government was weak in
the colonies (to speak of the most general circumstances
first) because the administration, that is, the executive,
lacked the flexibility it needed for successful engagement
in politics. The royal governors arrived in the colonies not
merely with a commission that outlined their duties but
with a book of instructions that filled in the details so
minutely and with such finality that in some of the most
controversial and sensitive public issues the executive was
in effect politically immobilized.[9] And what was true in
the crown colonies and in Massachusetts was true also,
if to a lesser extent, in the proprietary colonies. In the
whole area of maritime affairs, especially in matters
touching the enforcement of the navigation acts, the
actions of the governors were absolutely prescribed; they
were prescribed also in such other vital questions as the
issuance of paper money and the presumed obligation
of the Assemblies to grant permanent salaries to the chief
executives. Time after time on these and similar issues

---

[9] The Instructions have been edited and published in two
volumes by Leonard W. Labaree: *Royal Instructions to British
Colonial Governors, 1670–1776* (New York and London,
1935). For Professor Labaree's interpretation of their political
significance, see his *Royal Government,* pp. 30ff.

involving crown interests, the governors and their political allies would gladly have compromised,[10] but their instructions bound them. The result was that on many large and controversial issues the executive position was rigid, prescribed, and easily anticipated, and so while legally stronger and apparently more autocratic than it would otherwise have been, was by this fact alone politically weaker.

Yet even the strictest of instructions would not have been burdensome to the governors if they had had the equipment they needed, and which the government at home had in such abundance, to deal effectively with the politics of "the democracy" in a mixed government. The armory of political weapons so essential to the successful operation of the government of Walpole and Newcastle was reduced in the colonies to a mere quiverful of frail and flawed arrows.

Patronage was potentially the most effective weapon of all, and at the beginning of the provincial period the patronage at the disposal of governors was not negligible. In the course of half a century, however, it was so ground away by forces at either extreme of the political spectrum that ultimately the governors were left, in the words of one highly placed official lamenting his lack of gifts to bestow, "without the means of stopping the mouths of the demagogues." And later, after the Revolution, it would be commonly said in England and in loyalist circles that "the King and government of Great Britain held no patronage in the country, which

[10] On the salary question they most often did, commonly with the indulgence of the home government, the alternative being to receive no salary at all.

could create attachment and influence sufficient to
counteract that restless, arrogating spirit which in popular
assemblies, when left to itself, will never brook an authority that checks and interferes with its own." Originally
the governors held extensive powers of appointment to
military and civil offices. Though there were variations
from place to place, in most colonies the governors controlled the appointment of judges at all but the very
highest levels, including the local justices of the peace.
They controlled also the appointments of sheriffs, naval
officers, "and other necessary officers and ministers . . .
for the better administration of justice and putting the
laws in execution." Theirs too was the power of nomination, often tantamount to appointment, to the Council
seats. With these powers of appointment went the authority to dismiss or suspend incumbents in all these positions.[11]

[11] Anthony Stokes, *A View of the Constitution of the British
Colonies . . . at the Time the Civil War Broke Out on the
Continent of America . . .* (London, 1783), p. 138; William
Paley, *The Principles of Moral and Political Philosophy,* 7th
ed. (Philadelphia, 1788), p. 375; Evarts B. Greene, *The Provincial Governor in the English Colonies of North America*
(Cambridge, 1898), p. 111. So too, retrospectively, Governor
Dunmore of Virginia wrote, as the crisis of the Revolution
approached, that "if it had been thought fit to vest all the power
of this nature [i.e., patronage] which this government affords in
the hands of the governor, I should have had the means of
keeping down the attempts of party and faction which have
put the public affairs of this colony in the alarming situation
in which they actually stand." Dunmore to the Earl of Dartmouth, Dec. 24, 1774, quoted in Labaree, *Royal Government,*
p. 106. For specific enumerations of patronage powers in two
colonies, see Rex N. Naylor, "The Royal Prerogative in New
York, 1691–1775," *Quarterly Journal of the New York State
Historical Association,* 5 (1924), 221–251; and Albert B. Saye,
New Viewpoints in Georgia History (Athens, Ga., 1943), pp.
116–117.

There had been competition from England from the beginning. Appointment to the posts of chief justice, attorney general, auditor general, receiver general, and sometimes clerk of the Assembly was reserved to the English authorities throughout the eighteenth century. To this reserved list were added, from time to time, other positions. Appointment of the naval officers was taken over by the secretary of state for the southern department in the early eighteenth century by the simple device of issuing patent commissions that took precedence over all other such appointments, automatically replacing the incumbents—a practice that was complained of by colonial officials as early as the 1670's but used commonly nevertheless throughout the eighteenth century. Encroachments by the home authorities increased steadily as the political value in England of these far-flung, marginal, but still politically useful posts became clear. The climax came in 1752 when all of the colonial patronage except that directly under the control of the treasury and the admiralty was concentrated in the hands of the aggressive president of the Board of Trade, the Earl of Halifax, who for a time put its manipulation into a new high state of efficiency. But what was gained for the stability of politics in England was lost in America. The mere regularization of the colonial patronage in Halifax's hands reduced the political effectiveness of the administration in America.[12]

[12] Labaree, *Royal Government,* pp. 102, 104–105; Oliver M. Dickerson, *American Colonial Government, 1696–1765* (Cleveland, 1912), pp. 49, 142ff., esp. pp. 150–154; Arthur H. Basye, *The Lords Commissioners of Trade and Plantations* . . . (New Haven, 1925), pp. 71ff., esp. pp. 80–82.

The patronage forfeited by the governors to the home authorities was small, however, next to the losses that fell to the local political powers in the colonies. In some colonies encroachments on the governors' patronage were built into local institutions. Thus the Massachusetts charter required Council approval of gubernatorial appointments. More often encroachment resulted from the visible efforts of political opposition, and developed gradually. In Pennsylvania an act of the Assembly, in operation for many years before 1755, made all militia offices elective rather than appointive. In New Jersey and Maryland a local residence requirement was demanded, successfully, by the Assembly of all appointees to both civil and military positions. Virginia and Pennsylvania closely circumscribed the qualifications of those eligible for appointment as sheriff, in effect limiting the governors to selection from among local nominees; and four colonies restricted the tenure of sheriffs to stated periods of years. In several colonies the salaries of unpopular judges were withheld; in New York judicial salaries were granted annually judge by judge, as a means of influencing appointments. Everywhere after 1754 judicial commissions were issued only with the concurrence of the colonial Councils or a specified number of its members, an arrangement which, while meaningless in some colonies where the Councils were mere sounding boards for the governors, was in others an effective qualification on the governors' patronage powers.[13]

Most important of all of these encroachments on

[13] Greene, *Provincial Governor,* pp. 110–117.

the governors' patronage powers was the loss to the Assemblies almost everywhere of the power to fill the post of treasurer. Early concessions by the home authorities of the Assemblies' right to appoint to this crucial position, which controlled expenditures of public funds, were generalized in the early eighteenth century, with the result that the governor lost control not merely of these, in effect, local finance ministers, but also of the local political bosses, for the treasurers were everywhere persons of great political influence—pre-eminently so in the South where they doubled as speaker of the House. And the treasurers were only one of a range of revenue officers, control of whose appointments was contested by the lower houses. In South Carolina perhaps the greatest success was achieved, for here the governor lost control not only of the treasurer but of the commissary general, the comptrollers and receivers of the country duties, port waiters, powder receivers, and tax gatherers as well. Everywhere the governors complained with Arthur Dobbs of North Carolina, who was thoroughly harassed by a speaker-treasurer he said was at the head of "so great a party that [it] can lead the Assembly as [it] please[s]," that they "had not the power of rewarding [their] friends." As a result, the Board of Trade reported to the Privy Council in 1758, a governor "who [adheres] to the true principles of the constitution" found it impossible "to maintain His Majesty's just rights in America."[14]

[14] *Ibid.*, pp. 182–185; Labaree, *Royal Government,* pp. 300–301; Jack P. Greene, *The Quest for Power* (Chapel Hill, 1963), pp. 249–250, and chap. xi generally; William L. Saunders, ed., *The Colonial Records of North Carolina* (Raleigh, N.C.,

The thought pervades the writings of the royal governors, and of the proprietary governors as well. It was in proprietary Maryland, where the political use of patronage was perhaps more highly developed than elsewhere in the colonies, that the issue was most thoroughly aired. In 1760 two letters of extraordinary length—treatises, really—were exchanged between Governor Horatio Sharpe and the absentee secretary, Cecilius Calvert, over the possibility of "throwing out a sop in a proper manner to these noisy animals" in the lower House in the form of increased number of temporary offices carefully distributed so as to silence all possible opposition. The scheme, hatched in London, was impractical, Sharpe advised, for though he had long argued that, if it had been

His Lordship's pleasure to leave the disposal of all those offices that are not bestowed on councillors entirely to myself and to signify to those who may apply to him that he is determined to take notice of no applications for favor unless they come to him through my hands, I should flatter myself that in a few years many more of the delegates might be brought to act a moderate part [—though this much was true, he did not

1886–1890), III, 151; George Chalmers, *An Introduction to the History of the Revolt of the American Colonies* . . . (Boston, 1845), II, 361. The situation in Virginia was perhaps the most extreme: stripped entirely of influence over appointments at the county level and generally overridden by home authorities in appointments at the province level, "by 1740 the governor in Virginia was virtually without power to grant on his own either offices or favors . . . The governors' political patronage [had been reduced] to the status of a negative force in Virginia politics." David A. Williams, "Political Alignments in Colonial Virginia Politics, 1698–1750" (unpubl. diss., Northwestern Univ., 1959), pp. 249, 265.

think] that all the offices which are in the gift or disposal of the Lord Proprietary or his deputy . . . are
sufficient to secure a majority in the lower House . . .
That a great influence hath at times been gained in the
British House of Commons by such means is certain,
but it cannot be thence inferred that the same might be
easily done here.[15]

The difficulty of duplicating the English practice in
America was compounded by the adoption in the colonies
of Place Acts at least as strong in wording as the bills that
had finally, after long years of dispute, been adopted in
England. The authors of the New Jersey Place Act of
1730 first copied the exact wording of the relevant
passages of the English Place Act of 1707, with adapta-
tions for the local situation, and then, still unsatisfied that
they had dealt adequately with the problem, added:

That every person who, by reason of any office, pension, or salary from the crown, are by the laws of Great
Britain disabled to be elected or to sit or vote in the
House of Commons there, shall be and are hereby disabled to be elected or to sit or vote in any House of
Representatives hereafter to be summoned in this province . . .

In at least one colony the principle was taken further,
to the extreme position long since defeated in England, of
flatly excluding all officeholders from seats in the lower

[15] W. H. Browne, *et al.*, eds., *Archives of Maryland* (Baltimore, 1883–), IX, 377, 427, 429.

house whether or not their constituents were willing to re-elect them after their appointment.[16]

These provisions, incorporated after Independence in the first state constitutions, were later perceived to be obvious expressions of the American doctrine of the separation of powers. But in fact none of these provisions was written in response to that doctrine as we now understand it. They derive from an earlier intellectual context dominated not by the ideal of the balance of functioning branches of government but by the concept of mixed government and by a sense of the dangers it faced from "influence" and "corruption." The controlling ideas and attitudes were those of an anonymous pamphleteer who

[16] Betty Kemp, *King and Commons, 1660–1832* (London, 1959), pp. 54ff.; E. Neville Williams, ed., *The Eighteenth-Century Constitution, 1688–1815* (Cambridge, England, 1960), pp. 189–190; Samuel Allinson, comp., *Acts of the General Assembly . . . of New-Jersey . . . [1702–1776]* (Burlington, N. J., 1776), pp. 83–84; William W. Hening, ed., *The Statutes at Large . . . of Virginia . . .* (Richmond, etc., 1809–1823), IV, 292–293; Thomas Cooper and David J. McCord, eds., *The Statutes at Large of South Carolina . . .* (Columbia, S. C., 1836–41), III, 657 (cf. J. H. Easterby, ed., *The Journal of the Commons House of Assembly, February 20, 1744–May 25, 1745*, Columbia, S. C., 1955, pp. 34–36, 40); and especially the controversies in Maryland over a bill "to render any person incapable of a seat in the Lower House of Assembly that enjoys a place of profit from the Lord Proprietary," documented in *Archives of Maryland*, XXXIX, 159, 149–150; XLII, 107, 79, 80; XLIV, 622; XLVI, 271, 278, 216–217, 219; LVI, 176. Barker writes that the divergence between English and American practice revealed in the Maryland controversies over place acts, "—the Parliament, where the historic executive was weak, moving towards the domination of the executive; and the provincial legislature, where the historic executive was strong, moving towards a system of checks and balances—marks an early milestone in the history of institutional difference between America and Great Britain." *Background in Maryland*, p. 167.

lectured New Yorkers in 1732 on the importance of keeping the House of Representatives free from the corrupt influence of the governor. It was well known, he said, that corruption and the downfall of free governments result "from a prudent application of posts and pensions." A pension, he explained, "is a constant and continual bribe," pensioners being servants hired by the year "to do the dirty business of the House." A post, he added, "is a wet *pension,* and a *pension* is a dry post." And he ended this exposure of the threats to a free government as he had begun it, with a quotation from that universally popular paean to liberty, Addison's *Cato.*[17]

Thus the colonial governors were stripped of much of the power of patronage by which in England the administration could discipline dissent within the political community and maintain its dominance within Parliament. But it was not the existence of patronage alone that in England gave the administration its unique political advantage. The highly irregular, inequitable, and hence easily manipulated electoral system contributed greatly; and this too was absent in America.

There were no rotten boroughs in the colonies. No Assembly seats were owned outright by the government, and there were no spectral constituencies easily manipulated by the administration, for there had been no gradual accretion of "liberties" bestowed in ancient years in recognition of once-active but long since extinct political

[17] Charles R. Erdman, Jr., *The New Jersey Constitution of 1776* (Princeton, 1929), pp. 67–68; *O Liberty, Thou Goddess Heavenly Bright . . .* [New York, 1732; Evans no. 3595]. See, in general, Bernard Bailyn, *The Ideological Origins of the American Revolution* (Cambridge, 1967), pp. 70–72, and chap. vi, sec. 3.

forces. Though in Massachusetts any town, no matter how small, could send a representative to the General Court if it wished to, none below the level set for mandatory attendance ever did, and there is no indication that the governors ever attempted to impose themselves on the smaller hamlets with the intention of controlling their votes. They were not likely to have gained much if they had, for every town of forty voters was *obliged* to send a representative to the Assembly, and that body was therefore overwhelmingly controlled by country delegates. While in England the House of Commons was frozen in composition throughout the eighteenth century, most of the colonial assemblies, which were created at a stroke on general principles that implied unlimited growth—so-and-so-many delegates per unit of local government—were continuously expanding. So normal had the expectation of expansion become by mid-century that when governors, fearing the total eclipse of their influence in the legislatures by virtue of the increasing numbers of the country delegates, attempted to stop the multiplication of seats, they found themselves involved in serious political struggles; so too did local political leaders who sought to deny equal representation to expanding populations in the West. What is important is not that by enlightened twentieth-century American standards apportionment was here and there inequitable, but that by normal eighteenth-century standards it was remarkably equitable, well adjusted to the growth and spread of population and relatively insensitive, as a consequence, to pressure from an embattled executive.

The implications, for eighteenth-century ideas of

mixed government, of systems of representation flexibly adjusted to the growth and movement of population, were well understood at the time, clearly so by those like Governor Shirley of Massachusetts who attempted to stop the process and throw it back to a more static pattern. Thirty-three new towns, Shirley pointed out to the Board of Trade in 1743 in vetoing bills that created three additional new units of representation, had been created since the charter of 1691 went into effect. The result, he wrote, was that "the present number of the House of Representatives hath been sufficient to embarrass His Majesty's government here in some points though the most reasonable for them to comply with." The process of increasing the number of representatives should be stopped, he advised, especially since the power of "the democracy" expressed in the House of Representatives was already exaggerated by virtue of that body's chartered right of nominating the councillors. It is true, he wrote, that most of the towns consider representation more a burden than a benefit; ordinarily forty or fifty of the 160 qualified towns neglect to send representatives at all to the General Court. But that was not the point, he explained. These towns still

> . . . have it in their power upon an extraordinary emergency to double and almost treble their numbers, which they would not fail to do if they should be desirous of disputing any point with His Majesty's governor which they might suspect their ordinary members would not carry against his influence in the House.

He could easily point to examples of the effective use of this power against the interest of the crown, as could other governors seeking without the benefit of massive patronage some effective leverage against legislatures in which their interest was increasingly outweighed.[18]

The issue was not so clear-cut in all cases. In New York during the DeLancey regime in the 1750's, the situation was inverted, for in that case the lieutenant governor himself was the leading local politician, and his power was secure in the lower house. Elsewhere there were other variations. But everywhere the fact that representation was, if not equitable, either dynamic, growing, and changing with the growth and shifts in population, or embattled, because not sufficiently responsive to such movements, greatly complicated, if it did not render impossible, the reproduction in America of the pattern of "influence" which underlay the success of mixed government in England. In the end, but much too late, the problem was recognized in England for what it was. In 1767 the Privy Council, fearful of "too great an increase of the number and influence of the representative body, and . . . a disproportion to the other branches of the legislature," forbade governors to approve any bills that altered in any way the apportionment of representatives in the colonial Assemblies, thus abolishing at a stroke what Jefferson would characterize in the Declaration of Independence as "a right inestimable to [the people] and formidable to tyrants only."[19]

[18] *Acts and Resolves, Public and Private, of the Province of the Massachusetts Bay* . . . (Boston, 1869–1922), III, 70.
[19] William L. Grant and James Monro, eds., *Acts of the Privy Council of England, Colonial Series* (Hereford and London, 1908–1912), V, 33.

Apportionment was only one aspect of representation that created difficulties for the governors. Other practices created additional problems. From the earliest years it had been common in Massachusetts for towns to instruct their representatives how to act in the General Court in regard to controversial issues, and this practice continued into the eighteenth century, exercised irregularly, on occasions when the localities were committed to particular views they wished to have represented no matter what influence was brought to bear against their representatives. Elsewhere, too, representatives were instructed on delicate issues. In Maryland in 1754 a special convocation, called to consider repressive measures against the Catholics, declared it "to be the undoubted right of *British subjects* to instruct their representatives in such material points as may be the subject of their deliberations." Often when delegates were not instructed they themselves postponed acting until—as in New York in 1734—"they had taken the sentiments of their constituents."[20]

Instruction was but one form by which representation in the colonies was kept "actual," a form of attorneyship, as distinct from the virtual representation celebrated in Burke's description of Parliament as "a *deliberative* assembly of *one* nation, with *one* interest, that of the

[20] Kenneth Colegrove, "New England Town Mandates," *Publications of the Colonial Society of Massachusetts*, XXI (*Transactions*, 1919), 411–449; Barker, *Background in Maryland*, p. 254; William Smith, *History of the Late Province of New-York, from Its Discovery to . . . 1762*, II (*Collections of the New-York Historical Society* [vol. V] *for the Year 1830*, New York, 1830), 14.

whole, where, not local purposes, not local prejudices ought to guide, but the general good, resulting from the general reason of the whole." As well as being instructed by their constituents, delegates were required, often, to be actual residents of the communities they represented at the time of their incumbency. Residential requirements had not been common in the colonies in the seventeenth century. But since in America, a Pennsylvanian wrote in 1728, there was "no *transessentiating* or *transsubstantiating* of being from people to representative, no more than there is an absolute transferring of a title in a letter of attorney," such provisions increasingly appeared on the statutes. The result, the eighteenth-century historian William Smith wrote, was that the Assemblies seemed to be composed "of plain, illiterate husbandmen, whose views seldom extended farther than to the regulation of highways, the destruction of wolves, wildcats, and foxes, and the advancement of the other little interests of the particular counties which they were chosen to represent." Residential requirements were not universal in the eighteenth-century colonies, but they were commonly enough present to contribute measurably to the enfeeblement of "influence."[21]

[21] Burke's speech to the electors of Bristol, 1774; Roy N. Lokken, *David Lloyd* (Seattle, 1959), p. 232; Smith, *History of the Late Province of New-York*, I (*Collections of the New-York Historical Society* [vol. IV] *for the Year 1829*, New York, 1829), 309. Cf. Douglass' arguments for the abolition of Massachusetts' residential requirement, adopted in 1693: 1) "a gentleman of good natural interest and resident in the province, a man of reading, observation, and daily conversant with affairs of policy and commerce, is certainly better qualified for a legislator than a retailer of rum and small beer called

But of all the underlying characteristics that distinguished the process of politics in America from that of the English model, the breadth of the franchise was perhaps the most dramatic—and in its origins the most circumstantial. Like so many of the important conditions of the time, it had originally been neither planned nor desired; indeed, when it appeared it was not wholly understood for what it implied, nor used for political advantage to the extent that it might have been. Most colonies sought to do no more than re-create, or adapt with minor variations, the forty-shilling freehold qualification that had prevailed in the county constituencies of England for 300 years. But if ownership of land worth forty shillings a year was a restrictive qualification in England, it was permissive in the colonies where freehold tenure was almost universal among the white population. So weak a qualification was this traditional definition in the American context; so little did it serve to exclude from voting those who appeared to have been, in Blackstone's universally approved words, "in so mean a situation as to

---

a tavern keeper, in a poor obscure country town remote from all business"; 2) the typical "countryman will not be diverted from the most necessary and beneficial labor of cultivating the ground (his proper qualification) to attend state affairs, of which he may be supposed grossly and invincibly ignorant"; 3) "the poor township, by gentlemen at large serving gratis or generously as the quota of the township, will be freed from the growing . . . charge of subsisting an useless representative." *Summary*, I, 507. See in general the material assembled in Hubert Phillips, *The Development of a Residential Qualification for Representatives in Colonial Legislatures* (Cincinnati, 1921), which indicates that in nine of the mainland colonies representatives were required either by law or custom to be residents within their constituencies; and Bailyn, *Ideological Origins*, chap. v, sec. 1.

be esteemed to have no will of their own," that most colonies went on to specify the restriction more elaborately. But everywhere the effect was to broaden the franchise rather than to restrict it further. Some colonies defined the requirement in terms of acreage: in Virginia, one hundred acres unsettled, or twenty-five acres settled; in North Carolina and Georgia, fifty acres whether settled or unsettled. In New York and Virginia permanent or even lifetime leases were declared to be as good as freehold, and in several colonies personal property of any description, worth, in some places forty, in others fifty, pounds, was allowed to serve as qualification. Inflation of local currency values further eased the restrictions of franchise qualification. In Rhode Island a £400 property "restriction," measured in terms of local paper, opened the franchise to seventy-five per cent of the colony's adult males. To the disgusted Governor Thomas Hutchinson in Massachusetts it seemed that "anything with the appearance of a man" was allowed to vote.[22]

Generalizing across the variety of statutory provisions and practices of the various colonies, it seems safe to say that fifty to seventy-five per cent of the adult male white population was entitled to vote—far more than

[22] Chilton Williamson, *American Suffrage, from Property to Democracy, 1760–1860* (Princeton, 1960), chaps. i–iii (for the quotation from Blackstone, p. 11; for that of Hutchinson, p. 33); David S. Lovejoy, *Rhode Island Politics and the American Revolution, 1760–1776* (Providence, 1958), pp. 16–17. For details on the franchise in Massachusetts and Virginia, see Robert E. Brown, *Middle-Class Democracy and the Revolution in Massachusetts, 1691–1780* (Ithaca, 1955), and Robert E. Brown and B. Katherine Brown, *Virginia, 1705–1786: Democracy or Aristocracy?* (East Lansing, Mich., 1964).

could do so in England, and far more too, it appears, than wished to do so in the colonies themselves. Apathy in elections was common, in part because of the physical difficulty of travel to polling places; in part because of the lack of real alternatives in a society dominated by the sense that the natural social leaders of society should be the political leaders; in part because of the lack, in certain periods and places, of issues that seemed properly determinable at the polls. But however neglected, the wide-open franchise was potentially a powerful weapon, certain to work against the ability of the executives to control elections and hence to hold the line in the Assemblies for the interest of the state.

Yet even this does not exhaust the differences between the balance of forces in the English and American policies. Beyond all of these characteristics tending to deprive the colonial executive of the "influence" needed to duplicate the success of mixed government in England was the impermanency of the governors' tenure and the lack of finality of their decisions.

Gubernatorial appointments, as part of the patronage system of English politics, were susceptible to all of the vagaries, discontinuities, and irrationalities of that system. The determination of gubernatorial tenure had less to do with the shape of American political problems than with the exigencies of politics in England: it reflected at times the subtlest of adjustments in the most remote reaches of the English patronage network. Thus the fortunes of Jonathan Belcher of Massachusetts: appointed governor of his native province and of New Hampshire in

1730 by the influence of Charles, Viscount Townshend, Walpole's brother-in-law, he was deprived of that post in 1741 in part because his patron had been driven from the cabinet, in part because his rival, William Shirley, was able to manipulate, through his wife, an old acquaintance-ship with the Duke of Newcastle, but in greater part because Belcher's enemies were able to induce a devout London merchant to throw his electoral influence among the dissenters in the town of Coventry to a certain Lord Euston, favored by the administration, in exchange for the dismissal of Belcher.[23] Belcher's career was typical in its sensitivity to the movements of patronage politics in England, but it was atypical in its motivation. Belcher, unlike most governors in that he was American-born (only twenty per cent of all the royal governors in the whole of British America were American[24]), was content to pass his life in the colonial bureaucracy. Most governors, hoping to return to Britain after a profitable term of office in the colonies, were not; and thus accepted without rancor the uncertainties of tenure that were built into the system. But often it was more uncertain than even they had bargained for, and they found themselves cut off in mid-stream, before the expected benefits were gained. The problem was circular and self-intensifying. The mere

[23] John A. Schutz, "Succession Politics in Massachusetts, 1730–1741," *William and Mary Quarterly*, 3rd ser., 15 (1958), 508–520; Thomas Hutchinson, *The History of the Colony and Province of Massachusetts-Bay*, ed. Lawrence S. Mayo (Cambridge, 1936), II, 303.

[24] Leonard W. Labaree, "The Early Careers of the Royal Governors," *Essays . . . to Charles McLean Andrews by His Students* (New Haven, 1931), p. 148.

fact that they accepted office in America largely deprived them of the power to retain it, for by definition of his position the governor was removed from the sources of patronage and was out of contact with the forces capable of sustaining him in office. Only an absentee governor could be sure of eating his cake and having it too. Thus, as absentees the Earls of Orkney and Albemarle in succession held the governorship of Virginia for no less than fifty-seven consecutive years, from 1697 to 1754, during which time seven individuals came and went in the deputized office of lieutenant governor. The average duration of tenure of the fully appointed crown governors in the mainland colonies (excluding, that is, all lieutenant governors and all temporary incumbents) was five years, and of this period only the middle two or three years were effective politically, for a year or so was consumed at the start in consolidating power and an equivalent period of time was lost at the end when the incumbents were known to be lame ducks. Local political leaders were in little danger of being superseded. John Robinson was treasurer of Virginia for twenty-eight years; two brothers, Peyton and John Randolph, held the attorney generalship in succession from 1748 to 1776; two men held the speakership from 1738 to 1775. The average term of service of all the councillors in that province during the provincial period was 12.6 years, that of the burgesses in four counties examined for the period 1695–1769 (Gloucester, York, King and Queen, and Henrico) 8.2 years. If, Governor Spotswood wrote in 1718, the local political leaders in the Council win still another victory, "in the throwing out of a third governor, the country will be persuaded that they hold their places for life and the governor only during their pleasure."[25]

The brevity and uncertainty of tenure could have been better sustained by the governors had they had, during their effective years, the finality of decision needed to secure their authority. They soon discovered, if they did not realize in advance, the importance of the fact that there were two centers of executive authority, and that theirs was the less powerful of the two. On any issue at any time local opposition, frustrated by the actions of a determined executive, could go over the governor's head; turn his flank; get around behind him, by appealing directly to the higher authorities in England—authorities to which the opposition maintained, often, more permanent and reliable channels of communication than the governors. The governors were forced constantly, as a result, to look back over their shoulders, not merely to keep themselves in office but at times to secure their most ordinary decisions. There was, of course, a legal chain of command, and the governors had the inside track to the Board of Trade, the secretary of state for the southern department, and through them to the whole of English officialdom. But the official, formal table of organization often merely masked the real structure of influence.

[25] Labaree, *Royal Government*, p. 126; Charles S. Sydnor, *Gentlemen Freeholders*, pp. 96–97, and chap. vii generally; Spotswood to the Earl of Orkney, July 1, 1718, quoted in Williams, "Political Alignments in Colonial Virginia Politics," p. 187. For a revealing tabulation of the service of "The Leaders of the Lower Houses of Assembly in the Southern Royal Colonies, 1688–1776," see Greene, *Quest for Power*, App. III.

Politics in America was therefore profoundly different from politics in England in that it operated at two levels, the level of the provincial governments and the level of the central government at "home"; and it was the latter —more distant, less palpable, and less predictable— that was the more important. Americans had learned to live with this fact very early in their political history. By the mid-eighteenth century a stable pattern of informal communications had emerged, linking political forces in America directly to the political forces in England capable of overturning decisions taken in the colonies by the resident executive. There were, first, by the end of the first third of the century, the officially designated colonial agents who had developed into important official representatives of the Assemblies in England but whose informal lobbying was often more vital to the political concerns of the colonists than their official representations. And there were others more influential than they in the business of representing American interests directly in England. Almost everyone who attempted to manipulate English politics to the advantage of political groups in the colonies found it necessary at one time or another to work through professional political brokers, lawyers, commonly, who commanded the recondite legal knowledge and the subtle political lore needed to thread the dark passages of English politics. Sometimes these shadowy figures became powerful indeed. Thus a certain Ferdinand John Paris in the 1730's, while serving as the official London agent of the Penn family interests, represented also the Rhode Island and New Hampshire Assemblies, the East New Jersey Proprietors, the Georgia Trustees, the Mason family in its contest with Connecticut over certain land grants, several West Indian Assemblies, and the Morrisite faction in New York. Watching, as one can in Robert Hunter Morris' London diary, Paris' complicated maneuvering, one realizes the extent to which he, and others like him, were able to manipulate the political machinery of the English government.[26]

Equally effective at times in providing access to the sources of political power in England were channels that had been formed indeliberately, to serve other than simply political purposes. Commercial connections between merchants in England and in America often proved to be as valuable in politics as in trade. The Bakers, London merchants associated with the DeLanceys in New York in supplying goods for the illegal trade up the Hudson to Canada, helped establish the DeLancey influence in New York politics that lasted for almost thirty years. More important was the commercial syndicate led by John Thomlinson and involving subsequently George Hanbury and Barlow Trecothick. Thomlinson and Company—merchants, government contractors, and bankers—in its various permutations, had commercial interests throughout the Atlantic basin and especially in the northern mainland colonies; the group was close to the ministry and the main sources of patronage in the reign of George II. Their influence

[26] Beverly McAnear, ed., "An American in London, 1735–1736," *Pennsylvania Magazine of History and Biography*, 64 (1940), 164–217, 356–406; Mabel P. Wolff, *The Colonial Agency of Pennsylvania, 1712–1757* (Philadelphia, 1933), pp. 26ff.; Edward P. Lilly, *The Colonial Agents of New York and New Jersey* (Washington, D. C., 1936), pp. 176ff.

93

can be traced in innumerable ways in the politics of New England and the middle colonies. Solidly established in markets and sources of supply in the northern colonies, they could, if pressed, outmaneuver almost any governor who tried to oppose them, and when altogether unopposed, as in New Hampshire under the Wentworths, could create what no governor independently could conceivably have created, a perfectly integrated political machine, secured at every point from Whitehall to the western frontier. It would be largely their influence, later, dissipated at the accession of George III but in 1765–66 temporarily revived by the restoration to power of their old allies, the Rockinghams, that led the repeal of the Stamp Act.[27]

Religion too was important in securing informal links between native political forces in America and the sources of authority in London. Obviously the Church of England provided an effective system of political com-

[27] Lewis Namier and John Brooke, *The House of Commons, 1754–1790* (London, 1964), II, 39–41, III, 522–523, 557–560; Namier, *England in the Age of the American Revolution,* 2nd ed. (London, 1961), pp. 241–242, 246–250; Jere R. Daniell, "Politics in New Hampshire under Governor Benning Wentworth, 1741–1767," *William and Mary Quarterly,* 3rd ser., 23 (1966), 76–105. No consecutive account of Thomlinson's involvement in American politics and commerce has been written, but see, in addition to the above, John A. Schutz, *William Shirley* (Chapel Hill, 1961), and Joseph J. Malone, *Pine Trees and Politics* (Seattle, 1964). On the Canadian trade, see Jean Lunn, "The Illegal Fur Trade out of New France, 1713–60," Canadian Historical Association, *Report of the Annual Meeting . . . 1939,* pp. 61–76; and Charles H. McIlwain's Introduction to Peter Wraxall, *An Abridgment of the Indian Affairs [1754]* (Cambridge, 1915), chap. ii (especially pp. lxxiii–lxxiv nn).

munication for embattled Anglicans everywhere. The Church was used as a political agency not only in New England, where Anglicans were in effect dissenters and needed leverage against the Congregational establishment; and not only in New York, where vigorous nonconformist groups contested power with a fragmentary Anglican establishment; but also in Virginia, where Church leaders within a secure Anglican establishment battled local politicians—themselves Anglicans—who resisted executive claims to supremacy. What the Church of England provided elaborately, dissenting groups in England provided more simply and less reliably, but in some measure, nevertheless, did provide. American Baptists, Congregationalists, Presbyterians, and Quakers worked through co-denominationalists to force the levers of politics in England to their advantage in the colonies. And all of them took what benefit they could from the existence in England of a nonconformist lobby, the so-called Protestant Dissenting Deputies, that had been formed in and around London in 1732 primarily to force repeal of discriminatory legislation but that served dissenting interests more generally.[28]

Thus the configuration of circumstances: a deeply bred, firmly rooted assumption, reinforced by the appearance of institutions, that the colonial constitutions corresponded in their essentials to the prototypical mixed

[28] Carl Bridenbaugh, *Mitre and Sceptre* (New York, 1962), chaps. ii–vi.

government of England; an assumption, an expectation, violated in fact, first, by what were believed to be excessive powers, associated with Stuart autocracy, in the hands of the first order of the polity, and second, by the less clearly recognized but politically more important absence in the colonies of the cluster of devices by which in England the executive maintained discipline, control, and stability in politics. Swollen claims and shrunken powers, especially when they occur together, are always sources of trouble, and the malaise that resulted from this combination can be traced through the history of eighteenth-century politics.

But the structure of American politics in the eighteenth century is not wholly revealed in this. There are in addition distinctive characteristics of still another, even more fundamental, sort, that derive from the social substratum of politics.

The nature of leadership was different. Americans, like all Britons—indeed, like all Europeans of the eighteenth century—assumed that political leadership was only one of a number of expressions of leadership within society, and that it was in the nature of things that those who enjoyed superiority in one sphere would enjoy and exercise it in another. In the society of stratified "dignities" (if not classes) still considered in the eighteenth century to be normal or ideal, political leadership would devolve upon the natural social leaders of the community, whose identity, it was expected, would be steadily and incontestably visible. And so indeed it was in America—in *some* of the colonies, in *certain* respects, at *certain* times. In

Virginia this was to some extent the case once the upheaval of the 1670's was quieted; in the three generations that followed Bacon's Rebellion a hierarchy of the plantation gentry emerged in stable form, dominated by a social and economic leadership whose roots can be traced back to the 1650's and whose dominance in politics was largely uncontested. So too in Connecticut, a landed gentry of "ancient" families consolidated its control in the early eighteenth century and came to dominate the political life of the colony. But even in these extreme examples there were premonitions of disturbances that would eventually erupt—in Virginia in the almost limitless expansion of settlement in the west and the establishment there of new figures of potential power and of distinctive religious interests; in Connecticut in the growth of religious radicalism, especially in the eastern counties, already nervous and unsettled as a result of the leanness of the agricultural economy and of the frustrated desire for geographical expansion.[29]

Yet Virginia and Connecticut were colonies of the greatest stability. Elsewhere, the identity of the natural political leaders was seldom beyond contest, and at times was in itself the source of fierce political struggles. In New York this question lay at the heart of the Leislerian re-

[29] Bernard Bailyn, "Politics and Social Structure in Virginia," in James M. Smith, ed., *Seventeenth-Century America* (Chapel Hill, 1959), pp. 98–115; Jack P. Greene, "Foundations of Political Power in the Virginia House of Burgesses, 1720–1776," *William and Mary Quarterly,* 3rd ser., 16 (1959), 485–506; Sydnor, *Gentlemen Freeholders,* chaps. v–vii; Williams, "Political Alignments in Colonial Virginia Politics," chap. viii ("Seeds of Dissent, 1735–1749"); Oscar Zeichner, *Connecticut's Years of Controversy, 1750–1776* (Chapel Hill, 1949), chaps. i, ii.

bellion of 1689; the displaced Anglo-Dutch leadership "could not brook a submission to the authority of a man [Jacob Leisler] mean in his abilities and inferior in his degree."[30] So too in the seesawing series of displacements in authority of the Leislerians and the anti-Leislerians in the twenty years that followed, neither group acceded to the claims of leadership of the other; neither was sufficiently distinguished, sufficiently in control, to rule without contest. Elections were frequently conceded in the counties of New York, but leadership was never beyond contest.[31] There and elsewhere new figures appeared overnight, from nowhere and everywhere, to enter the arena of politics. In Massachusetts, the Apthorps appeared from the West Indies and New York; the Hancocks, from Lexington; the Belchers, from Cambridge; the Otises, from Barnstable; the Adamses, from Boston and Braintree. And always there were alien elements introduced into the top of the political hierarchy in the form of officials sent from England in positions of high authority.

The mere existence of this uncertainty in leadership was in itself a source of political disturbance. But the

[30] Smith, *History of New York*, I, 86.

[31] Thus, though the unknown schoolteacher William Forster later apologized for running against the recently displaced chief justice and veteran political boss Lewis Morris in the Westchester election of 1733 ("He hoped the late judge would not think the worse of him for setting up against him") and though Morris replied *"that he was highly blamable"* for doing so, Forster had had no hesitation in defying the Westchester establishment, and in fact polled 151 votes out of 420 cast. *New York Weekly Journal*, Nov. 5, 1733. On the political independence generally of the tenants on the New York estates, see Milton M. Klein, "Democracy and Politics in Colonial New York," *New York History*, 40 (1959), pp. 229–232.

social conditions it reflected contributed even more to the incidence and persistence of faction. Leadership was uncertain largely because the economy was uncertain. The interests that sought expression in politics varied and shifted. Rhode Island was never a tranquil colony. Indeed, there was turmoil in Rhode Island even before the colony legally existed. But though controversy continued in the eighteenth century, especially when paper money was at issue, politics was relatively calm, until in the 1750's the opening of a new entrepôt for agricultural goods at the head of Narragansett Bay and the associated emergence of ambitious merchant farmers seeking the benefits of government in the exploitation of this new source of supply, blew the existing arrangements skyhigh and pitched the colony into a political upheaval that lasted for eight years.[32] So too, though less dramatically, the town of Baltimore suddenly emerged from nowhere in the mid-1740's to become in less than a decade one of the major American commercial centers, supported by the agricultural surpluses of a freshly developing hinterland; overnight the town and the surrounding region produced a new group of merchants and became a new base of political influence.[33] So too the opening of the western Virginia lands to tobacco cultivation gave rise to new elements in Virginia politics. The openness of the economy led to repeated innovations and displacements

[32] Mack Thompson, "The Ward-Hopkins Controversy . . ." *William and Mary Quarterly*, 3rd ser., 16 (1959), 363–375; cf. Lovejoy, *Rhode Island Politics*, pp. 6ff.

[33] Clarence P. Gould, "The Economic Causes of the Rise of Baltimore," *Essays to Charles McLean Andrews*, pp. 234ff.

that sought expression in politics. There were no "classes" in colonial politics, in the sense of economic or occupational groups whose political interests were entirely stable, clear, and consistent through substantial periods of time. More important, there was not sufficient stability in the economic groupings more loosely defined to re-create in America the kind of stable interest politics that found in England so effective an expression in "virtual" representation. Samuel Beer's description of the economic reality behind the dominant concept of representation in eighteenth-century England is relevant, by contrast, to the equivalent reality in America. Burke's, and the Old Whigs's view of representation, Professor Beer writes, assumed that the interests considered legitimate in politics were not individual people but corporate bodies:

> local communities united by ancient ties of interest [and] . . . broad social groupings . . . —the various "estates," "ranks," "orders" and—to use the term most commonly employed—"interests," of which the nation and the empire were composed. Not individuals but such functional groupings were the basic units of representation along with the local communities. Hence, virtual representation was possible; the M.P. from Bristol, for example, virtually represented not only that city, but also all other places which did not have actual representation in Parliament, but which, as out-ports and centers of shipping and commerce, had common interests with Bristol.

Though economic groups sought expression in the colonial Assemblies, there were no "functional groupings" in this English sense in pre-Revolutionary America. The economy was too immature, too fresh, too easily exploited, too quickly developing, too shifting, and too unreliable for that.[34]

An indeterminate leadership and an unstable economic structure were powerful generators of conflict in communities whose ideal was a static polity and whose presumption was that the essential groupings of social forces were in some sense reasonably described by the terms monarchy, aristocracy, and democracy. But the sources of factionalism lay deeper even than this. Ultimately they involved the role of government in society; and again, the contrast with England is instructive. The purpose of the general government in eighteenth-century England, Richard Pares has written, was not to legislate but simply "to govern: to maintain order, to wage war and, above all, to conduct foreign affairs." When foreign affairs were calm "there was nothing to think about . . . but the control and composition of the executive government itself. Indeed, when there is nothing to do but to govern, no other subject is worth thinking about." Parliament did, of course, pass some laws relating to social and economic development, "but most of this legisla-

[34] Samuel H. Beer, "The Representation of Interests in British Government: Historical Background," *American Political Science Review*, 51 (Sept., 1957), 617–618. Thus an anonymous writer ("The Watchman") wrote in the *Pennsylvania Journal*, April 27, 1758: "We see, then, how erroneous and dangerous a prejudice, too common in the country, is which asserts that the *merchants* and *farmers* have distinct and opposite interests, whereas in truth one common interest connects both." The article attempts to demonstrate at length the interdependence of the two major interests in Pennsylvania.

tion was private, local, and facultative, setting up local agencies, such as turnpikes, paving, enclosure, or improvement commissioners where such things appeared to be desired by the preponderant local interests." Such matters were not the concern of public but of private legislation. "The work of the British Government was virtually restricted to preserving the constitution (which meant doing nothing in home affairs) and conducting foreign policy."[35]

This was not the case in America. For though it is true that the colonial legislators thought no more in terms of legislative programs than did Members of Parliament, it is also true that the colonial legislatures were led willy-nilly, by the force of circumstance, to exercise creative powers, and in effect to construe as public law what in England was "private, local and facultative." For there devolved upon them, out of the necessity of the situation, the power of controlling the initial distribution of the primary resource of the society: land. Whether in their own names, as in the chartered colonies, or in the name of higher authority, as in the royal and proprietary colonies, the colonial governments in one or another of their branches came to exercise this essential power; much of colonial politics was concerned with the efforts of individuals and groups to gain the benefits of these bestowals.[36]

[35] Richard Pares, *George III and the Politicians* (Oxford, 1953), pp. 4, 5, 3; John Brooke, "Introductory Survey," in Namier and Brooke, *House of Commons, 1754–1790*, I, 184.

[36] For a particularly vivid and detailed account of the politics of land distribution, see Edith M. Fox, *Land Speculation in the Mohawk Country* (Ithaca, 1949).

Control of the distribution of land, so crucial in the wilderness setting of eighteenth-century America, was merely one of a number of powers which fell to the colonial governments by virtue of the newness of the society and of the urgency of rapid development. A range of public facilities, which in more settled communities had come into being gradually in the course of innumerable private and public efforts, had here to be created abruptly. Immunities and benefits had to be bestowed—to build wharfs, roads, ferries, public vessels, civic buildings—in numbers and with a suddenness that had no parallel in the settled society of England until the full impact of the industrial revolution was felt.[37] And not only material facilities: social institutions too had to be

---

[37] Frederick H. Spencer, *Municipal Origins, An Account of English Private Bill Legislation . . . 1740–1835* . . . (London, 1911), summary, pp. 2–3, and *passim*; Sidney and Beatrice Webb, *English Local Government: Statutory Authorities for Special Purposes* (London, 1922); William Holdsworth, *A History of English Law*, X (London, 1938), pp. 188ff. Cf. Lucille Griffith, *Virginia House of Burgesses, 1750–1774* (Northport, Ala., 1963), p. 211, where it is shown that about sixty per cent of the laws passed in Virginia were acts pertaining to social and economic problems; and Sirmans, *Colonial South Carolina*, p. 244: "Such diverse matters as the regulation of lawyers' fees, building codes for Charles Town, the conduct of seamen, regulation of merchandising, the tenure of church pews, and a program of farm subsidies came within the purview of the assembly." South Carolina is perhaps the most extreme example since "there was little local government in South Carolina, and the assembly had to become involved in such matters as the operation of ferries and the construction and repair of churches." But even where local government was strong, as in Massachusetts, the tradition of governmental intervention in the economy was well established, and the government's response to enterprising individuals and grou~ ~was positive.

created, or legalized. Towns had to be established by writ of the governments, schools provided for in legislation, and colleges chartered. Laws, too, had to be devised which in effect decreed ease or distress, if not life or death, for religious institutions in communities where the mere variety of groups ruled out an easy acceptance of what was orthodox and what was not. So in New York the presumed right of the government to bestow its favor on an Anglican college was the source of one of the most celebrated political battles of the century.[38] The benefits of government were magnified where so little existed and where so much had to be created so quickly.

Since government is power, its control will always be a matter of contention. The involvement of the government in the process of development was in itself a source of conflict, and it tended to intensify controversies that otherwise existed.

Such were the shaping elements of those "noisy dissatisfactions" that so plagued the tranquillity of governors in eighteenth-century America: an apparent excess of jurisdiction in the hands of the first—the executive or monarchical—order of what were presumed to be mixed and balanced governments, coupled incongruously with a severe reduction of the "influence" available to the executive—"influence" which in England allowed the govern-

[38] William Livingston, *et al.*, *The Independent Reflector*, ed. Milton M. Klein (Cambridge, 1963), pp. 20–48; Beverly McAnear, "American Imprints Concerning King's College," *Papers of the Bibliographical Society of America*, 44 (1950), 301–339.

ment to enforce its authority, and discipline and control the whole of the polity; and a social and economic order that blurred the expected distinctiveness of political leadership, prevented the settlement of stable interest groups, and drew the government closely into the process of development. The result was a political system which in any case would be troubled and contentious. In the context of Anglo-American political culture of the mid-eighteenth century it became something more than that: it became explosive. For it evoked in their most extreme forms both the deeply bred belief that faction was seditious, a menace to government itself, and the fear, so vividly conveyed by the radicals and the virulent anti-"Robinarchs" in England, that the government was corrupt and a threat to the survival of Liberty.

THE LEGACY

I HAVE SUGGESTED that a paradox lay at the heart of provincial politics in eighteenth-century America: on the one hand an enlargement, beyond what was commonly thought compatible with liberty, of the legal authority possessed by the first branch of government, the executive; and on the other hand, a radical reduction of the actual power in politics exercised by the executive, a reduction accounted for by the weakness of the so-called "influence" by which the crown and its ministers in England actually managed politics in that country. At once regressive and progressive—carrying forward into the Augustan world powers associated with Stuart autocracy yet embodying reforms that would remain beyond the reach of reformers in England for another century or more—American politics in the mid-eighteenth century was a thoroughgoing anomaly. Conflict was inevitable: conflict between a presumptuous prerogative and an over-great democracy, conflict that had no easy resolution and that raised in minds steeped in the political culture of eighteenth-century Britain the specter of catastrophe.

Everywhere but in the corporate enclaves of Connecticut and Rhode Island one finds a record of such conflict, generated by a political system that was anomalous in its essence. Everywhere the basic forces at work were the same, but everywhere local circumstances gave particular shape to the resulting politics. It is to these distinctive configurations in the separate colonies, to this mingling of regressive and progressive elements in various combinations at specific times and places, that one must turn before examining directly the explosive amalgam of politics and ideology that resulted from these pressures— and that is the ultimate legacy of these years.

****

N ew York's history is an almost ideal type—its leading figures are vivid exemplars—of this immoderate politics. For twenty-five years after the Glorious Revolution New York was the scene of violently rocketing factionalism touched off by the *coup d'état* of Jacob Leisler, an ambitious, prickly German who in 1689 managed to upset the control of the dominant group of Anglo-Dutch merchants and landowners, and replaced it with a shambling quasi-military junto of lesser figures: ambitious men hitherto subordinated—in several cases proscribed—by the swiftly risen but still quite insecure ruling clique. The anti-Leislerians, favored by the avaricious Governor Benjamin Fletcher, rioted in the spoils of office and plundered their defeated enemies; when the tide turned under the governorship of Lord Bellomont they were attacked with equal violence. Neither side in office could control the "popular" forces in the Assembly; their efforts to do so led to notable advances in the claims of "the democracy" in the Lower House. Nor, in the tumultuous politics of pre-Hanoverian England, could either secure their support perfectly at home. Extremism grew at both ends of the political spectrum, irrespective of which group happened to occupy which end. Both sides when in control of the administration went so far beyond the usual claims of prerogative as to attempt judicial murder; both sides out of office championed the cause of liberty, sought to extend representation, to bind representatives more tightly to their constituencies, and to enlarge the power of the House. Peace came only under the adroit management of Governor Robert Hunter, whose unique success in calming for a time the colony's tumultuous factionalism is as revealing of the underlying problems of colonial politics as are his predecessors' failures.

Hunter was a gifted politician as well as a sophisticated courtier: like so many of the early eighteenth-century crown governors in America he had fought under Marlborough at Blenheim; but he was no ordinary "army" man. An accomplished belletrist, friend and correspondent of Addison and Swift, in the midst of his embroilments in New York he wrote a high-spirited, scabrous parody of American politics that must have delighted his friends at home.[1] His settlement of 1717 was managed for him by that typical eighteenth-century creole politician, Lewis Morris. Avid for distinction and power, unequaled, a contemporary reported,

---

[1] *Androborus* ([New York], 1714). No full account of Hunter's remarkable career has been written. The best summary of his political management in New York is in Charles W. Spencer, *Phases of Royal Government in New York 1691–1719* (Columbus, O., 1905); see also Herbert L. Osgood, *The American Colonies in the Eighteenth Century* (New York, 1924–25), II, chap. xix. For some vivid reminiscences of Hunter by Cadwallader Colden, including anecdotes of Hunter's earlier years which Colden had direct "from Mr. Hunter's mouth, with every particular circumstance which attended them," see Colden's letters to his son, 1759, in *Collections of the New-York Historical Society for the Year 1868* (New York, 1868), pp. 192ff.

in "the arts of intrigue," Morris was endlessly scrabbling for gain, shuffling nervously for position in an unstable world, and disciplined to pursue to the last wearisome turn the petty intrigues that surrounded him. The Hunter-Morris settlement resulted from the successful effort to manufacture a dominant gubernatorial "interest." The administration made strenuous efforts, first, to elect their supporters to the Assembly; six seats were won at the polls for the governor's interest. Five more were added by the creation of new' constituencies, under constitutional provisions originally devised by the Leislerians, and by the enlargement of existing electoral districts. Victory was finally secured by the introduction of a patronage system by which, a contemporary explained, governors "to serve their purposes in election . . . grant, as it is called, the administration to particular favorites in each county, which is the nomination of officers, civil and military." By 1716, the historian William Smith reported, "the harmony introduced between the several branches of the legislature" was clear evidence "that the majority of the House were now in the interest of the governor." Hunter's chief opponent, the speaker of the House, forthwith resigned his position, "disgusted," it was said, "with the governor's prevailing interest in the House."[2]

The Hunter-Morris settlement brought peace to New York after decades of vicious factionalism. But its roots did not lie

[2] William Smith, *The History of the Late Province of New-York from Its Discovery to the Appointment of Governor Colden, in 1762,* I (*Collections of the New-York Historical Society* [vol. IV], *for the Year 1829,* New York, 1829), pp. 180, 310, 199, 200. On Morris, like Hunter an important type-figure, see Gordon B. Turner, "Governor Lewis Morris and the Colonial Government Conflict," *Proceedings of the New Jersey Historical Society,* 67 (1949), 260–304. Of the various accounts of eighteenth-century New York politics I have relied most heavily on Stanley N. Katz's forthcoming book, *Newcastle's New York: Anglo-American Politics, 1732–1753,* which he kindly allowed me to consult in manuscript; I have profited also from his criticism of a draft of these lectures.

deep in the political soil, and it could not be sustained; it is less surprising that it was destroyed than that it survived as long as it did. Pressure against the Hunter-Morris settlement began to build up almost immediately from sources of opposition both in the colony and in England. Morris and his new patron, Governor William Burnet (the bishop-historian's son, in New York to recover his losses in the South Sea Bubble), were so fearful that a slight dislodgment would pitch the government into an abyss of faction that they refused flatly to call for new elections. They refused first on the likely occasion of Burnet's arrival (a refusal instantly declared to be part of "an anti-constitutional project"); they refused again, against a sharply rising clamor of opposition, at the even more likely occasion of the end of a triennial period; and they refused again, now against outraged opinion, at the expiration of the septennium. But the end was in sight. The narrow limits of patronage had been reached, and losses in by-elections had shaved Morris' legislative margin paper thin. Above all, there was no way of blocking the emergence into politics of a powerful new competitive interest that had first appeared after the peace of Utrecht.

The economic strength of the Morris-Hunter group had lain in its near-monopoly of the Indian trade managed through retail trading houses established in the adjacent Indian territory, which excluded from the richest profits a group of merchants specializing in the quasi-legal wholesale trade with the French in Canada. Burnet and Morris outlawed the Canadian trade by stringent new laws, which they succeeded in having endorsed in England. This helped in the end to destroy them. The DeLanceys in New York, committed to the Canadian trade from which they had profited during the war, found support in London from a syndicate of export merchants led by Samuel Baker. With this backing they joined with the Philipse family, then the leaders of the opposition in the Assembly, to create an overwhelming anti-administration interest. Pressure for what could only be a critical election built up year after year, and in 1727 the administration could resist no longer. An election was called, and the Morrisites were decisively defeated. Within a year the whole edifice of Hunter's and Morris' carefully constructed "influence" was obliterated; within two years the Morris-Burnet trade policy was reversed, and Burnet himself, his personal position untenable, was forced out of office to make room for a former groom of the bedchamber of George II. In 1728 Burnet left New York for the governorship of Massachusetts, where he was instantly engaged by an even more articulate and less manageable opposition than the one that had defeated him in New York. He died a year after his arrival in Massachusetts, destroyed by a faction whose power he could not control. In one of his last communications to Newcastle he wrote of his desperation, and asked—as would, fatally, another governor in similar circumstances forty years later—for the dispatch to Boston of two companies of troops to shore up his faltering authority.

In New York, following Burnet's departure, Morris, the least egalitarian of men, threw himself more and more upon popular support, voicing increasingly radical propositions phrased more and more distinctly in the words of the extreme libertarians in England. While the governor's party turned increasingly to devices associated with autocratic rule—the use of prerogative courts, reminiscent of the reign of Charles I, created and maintained by executive order; the dismissal of judges, as in the reign of James II, deemed politically unreliable; the silencing of opposition on charges of seditious libel (for utterances indistinguishable from those regularly hurled at Walpole) —while the administration was using such devices, the Morrisite opposition exploited the most radical potentialities of the colonial situation. Their savage assaults on the Cosby administration set in motion events that culminated in Morris' dismissal from the chief justiceship and in the world-famous trial of their printer, John Peter Zenger. In the end, after defeating in the well publicized Westchester election of 1734 a gubernatorial candidate who had run with all the support, legal and illegal, that could be given him by the governor's allies, Morris left New York for London, where he hoped to recover his personal losses if not to destroy his enemies by currying favor at the ultimate source of power. In a series of maneuvers graphically recorded in the diary of his son, Robert Hunter Morris, he won a partial victory, and then turned to new avenues of advancement, not in New York but in New Jersey, to which in 1738 he returned as governor. With his appointment to New Jersey the Morrisite faction in New York, formed twenty-five years earlier as the administration party of Robert Hunter, trailed away to inconsequence.

Their ultimate successors, the DeLanceys, had much earlier laid the basis in England for the power they would eventually exercise in New York. When fully elaborated, the network of ties the DeLanceys were able to maintain could absorb harmlessly almost any assault pitched against it in England. Their alliances included not only the Baker mercantile syndicate, now shoulder-deep in the quasi-legal Canadian trade which the DeLanceys managed for them in New York, and their in-laws, the Heath-cotes, highly influential in trade and politics on both sides of the Atlantic, but also the Archbishop of Canterbury, who had been James DeLancey's college tutor, and the powerful admiral, Sir Peter Warren, who when captain of the British station ship in New York harbor had married James DeLancey's sister. It was the Baker-Warren combination that reduced Governor George Clinton to helplessness when he attempted to enforce the ministry's war plans against the interests of the Canadian traders; and it was through the same set of influences that James De Lancey obtained the reversion of the lieutenant governorship upon Clinton's retirement in 1753. But if the DeLanceys were able to secure their political position at the English end of the political system, they remained vulnerable at the other. To increase their interest they challenged the law, originally introduced by the Leislerians as a weapon against Fletcher's administration, requiring representatives to be residents of their constituencies, but they succeeded only in reaffirming the general opinion that, "contrary to legal exposition and Parliamentary usage . . . a personal residence was as requisite in the elector as communion of interests by a competent freehold."[3] Earlier, James DeLancey's associate, Cosby's successor Lieutenant Governor George Clarke, had attempted to placate the opposition by conceding several important points to the Assembly, but all he accomplished by this was to embolden his antagonists to flood the legislature with radical proposals—proposals for making triennial elections mandatory; for regulating elections so as formally to exclude all possibility of gubernatorial influence; for stripping crown officials of their fees; and for making appropriations forever after annual. Clarke's ultimate solution had at least been safe: he left America in 1745, returning to the Somerset countryside he had left forty-two years before to make his fortune, under powerful patronage, as a colonial official. Others in his position were less fortunate. Governor Clinton's immediate successor, Sir Danvers Osborn, hoping in America to overcome his grief at the death of his wife and incidentally to recoup his dwindling fortune, arrived in 1753 with stringent instructions, written by Charles Townshend —instructions which Horace Walpole described as "better calculated for the latitude of Mexico and for a Spanish tribunal. than for a free rich British settlement"—to maintain prerogative power absolutely. A brief inspection of the province convinced him, in the historian Smith's words, "that his administration would not only prove destructive to his private fortune but draw upon him the general odium of the country, and excite tumults dangerous to his personal safety."[4] Five days after his arrival in New York he committed suicide.

[3] Smith, *History of the Late Province of New-York,* II (*Collections of the New-York Historical Society* [vol. V], *for the Year 1830,* New York, 1830), p. 40.

[4] Lewis Namier and John Brooke, *Charles Townshend* (London, 1964), p. 37; Smith, *History of the Late Province of New-York,* II, 160.

The DeLanceys were never able simultaneously to maintain control in England and eliminate opposition in New York. It was in the 1750's, when the DeLancey power was at its height, that one of the bitterest factional fights of the eighteenth century broke out: the dispute between the DeLanceys and the so-called Presbyterian Party, led by William Livingston, William Smith, Jr., and John Morin Scott, over the founding of the proposed Anglican college in the province. In the course of this wildly ramifying struggle for what amounted to control of the province's politics, the DeLancey forces were harassed in the Assembly, outvoted at the polls, and subjected to public vilification matched only by the torrents of abuse the Morrisites had poured on Cosby twenty years before. James DeLancey, chief justice, lieutenant governor, and political boss, was too shrewd to insist openly on his right to exercise the extraordinary powers to which he was entitled by law. But the powers of his position were unmistakably autocratic and the opposition responded, in speeches in the Assembly and in pages of the *Independent Reflector* and the other opposition publications, with arguments, rebuttals, and proposals more advanced than anything heard in influential political circles in England at any time in the eighteenth century—or, in fact, in the nineteenth century too.

Politics in this one colony—delicately balanced, riven with conflict—was paralleled with variations in the other colonies. In **Massachusetts** for the first forty years of the eighteenth century there was the same conflict between a legally overgreat but politically weak executive and an implacable, assertive "democracy." Through the administrations of Dudley, Shute, Burnet, and Belcher (1702–41) the governors sought to impose their wills on an entrenched opposition and consolidate the government under their own leadership. But they were bound by instructions that smacked of excessive prerogative. Their unambiguous instructions to extract from the Assemblies permanent and irrevocable grants of salaries were felt to be a throwback to claims that had been denied—once and for all, it had been thought—in the reign of Charles I. Their insistence on controlling election to the House speakership invoked a power that had been refused William III in 1695 and that had not, in England, been claimed by the crown thereafter. Their repeated vetoes of Assembly-elected members of the Council appeared to rob the House of the strength it needed to maintain a proper balance in a constitution overweighted, it was believed, by prerogative power. Laws were vetoed, Assemblies prorogued and dissolved when advantageous to the governor, and rights of property, it was felt, were threatened by attempts to enforce the crown's monopoly of mast timber deep in the interior.

But though the governors claimed and attempted to exercise these overgreat powers, their political influence was in fact small. Dudley, a shifty, unpopular local politician turned English placeman, was never able to overcome the opposition led by the Ashursts in England and the Cookes in Massachusetts, both of whom had opposed his appointment in the first place and whose economic interests clashed in part with his. He managed to keep the support of the Boston merchants whose interests in military contracting he favored, and by the careful use of limited patronage maintained a semblance of discipline in the Assembly; but he never fully controlled the House and could not prevent its accusing him and his confederates of complicity with the enemy and of profiteering. The battle between the governor and the popular forces in the House and Council was continuous, and when the opposition broadened over the land bank issue and Dudley's support in England fell away with a change in ministries, the governor was easily disposed of. Shute's and Burnet's administrations were even less successful. The opposition, swollen by the animosities created by the salary, land bank, and timber rights issues, proved to be unmanageable. The two hapless governors scarcely even tried "to form an interest within the House itself in support of the just claims of the executive." Administration and opposition, locked in a struggle neither could win, lectured each other continuously in the Assembly and in pamphlet and newspaper exchanges, and concluded by issuing mutually contradictory interpretations of the British constitution. Belcher was more energetic politically and more knowledgeable about New England, but though he was able to conclude the salary question (by accepting defeat) "he was not fully in control of local politics because many key men in the administration were not personally loyal to him and because his uncertain standing at home was well known in Boston. In addition, he had not enough offices to distribute, not enough power to settle problems of finances and administration, and not enough control over the legislature to guide its policies." A slow and careful build-up of opposition groups, managed by an adroit, fortune-hunting lawyer, William Shirley, whom Belcher had befriended and whose career he had advanced, climaxed in 1741 when the governor, incapable of defeating the Land Bankers' interest in the House, launched in desperation a purge of the Bank supporters from all positions in the government. It was a disastrous move, and it ended his usefulness as governor; his support, both in Massachusetts and in England, fell away, and he was forthwith replaced in office by Shirley.[5]

"I am now entering upon the government of a province," Shirley wrote at the start of his long administration (1741–1757), "where Colonel Shute quitted the chair and Mr. Burnet broke his heart through the temper and opposition of the people; and Mr. Belcher in the midst of his countrymen failed of carrying any one of those points for the crown which might have been expected from him." Shirley's success, like Hunter's in New York, was based on carefully calculated concessions to local political interests, and it was richly favored by circumstance. His success was made possible largely by the wars that occupied most of the

[5] Osgood, *American Colonies in the Eighteenth Century,* III, 160; John A. Schutz, "Succession Politics in Massachusetts, 1730–1741," *William and Mary Quarterly,* 3rd ser., 15 (1958), 511.

sixteen years of his administration. It was the patronage, the long "chain of favors," created by the military operations in the northern American theater of war that enabled him to control the political system in Massachusetts. Effective distribution of offices, commissions, and contracts was throughout his administration the first order of business. His position weakened only when demobilization reduced the gifts he could bestow, for the normal condition of politics still favored the opposition and made it possible for "popular" forces to paralyze the efforts of any aggressive administration. When in the end Shirley's ambitions broadened beyond Massachusetts and led him at the apogee of his career to assume the command of the British military forces on mainland America, he failed, his biographer writes, because "he lacked the power to control the patronage of New York, Pennsylvania, and Virginia." Even in Massachusetts his control was never perfect. He had at one point to solicit the support of the home authorities in denying representation to newly created townships in order to preserve his precarious majority in the House. It was when he was at the height of his power, in 1748–49, that he was faced with the most vicious and most articulate opposition he ever had to deal with; his opponents' short-lived journal, *The Independent Advertiser,* edited or managed by James Allen and William Douglass, is identical in opposition animus, tone, and ideas to Zenger's *New York Weekly Journal.* It too lifted almost all its theoretical statements verbatim, though without attribution, from the pages of *Cato's Letters.* Shirley, like Cosby fifteen years earlier in New York, considered prosecuting the opposition for seditious libel, but wisely pulled back at the last moment.[6]

The pattern of politics in the proprietary colonies was different in form but not in substance. **Pennsylvania,** as the eighteenth-century annalist Proud wrote, was never "without a dis-

[6] John A. Schutz, *William Shirley* (Chapel Hill, 1961), pp. 49, 84, 268, 133; cf. above, p. 82.

contented and murmuring party . . . who thought it their duty and interest constantly to oppose the Proprietary, in all cases indiscriminately, where either his power or interest was concerned; and though frequently but small and weak, yet they were sufficiently able to embarrass the public proceedings and endanger the general tranquillity." Clashes that would by 1744 make of the Pennsylvania government "a kind of anarchy (or no government)" began among the Quakers in the earliest years of the eighteenth century when the "country party" opposition, led by the fiercely belligerent Welshman David Lloyd, threw itself against every effort of Penn's faithful agent, James Logan, and his following to advance the interests of the proprietors and the Quaker merchants and to support the authority of the executive. Secure in the control of the House, the opposition, raising "that popular and plausible cry, of standing for *liberties* and *privileges*," condemned a succession of proprietary governors and agents as autocrats, and repeatedly paralyzed the government in efforts to advance popular causes: to eliminate vice-admiralty jurisdiction (a worse threat to liberty, Lloyd said, than Charles I's ship money); to confine the supreme judicial power to the Assembly; to eliminate the veto power of the proprietor; to maintain the Assembly's control of judicial tenure and of its own convening and proroguing; and to strip the Council of effective power. A generation later personalities and immediate issues had changed, but the now Anglican proprietary-executive forces, enfeebled by constitutional limitations and the lack of patronage and popular support in the annual elections, were still condemned as autocratic and harassed at every turn by an indefatigable opposition that warned ceaselessly of the proprietors' intention "to seize power by encroaching on the constitutional representation of the people and by establishing a vast system of patronage." The famous "Quaker party" of the 1740's and '50's, which controlled the House and local offices and defied the proprietary interest in a series of violent clashes first over support of the war effort and then over taxing proprietary lands and eliminating the Pennsylvania charter, was the latter-day expression of a disposition of political forces as old as the colony itself.[7]

In **The Carolinas** conflict was even more deep-seated. The Proprietors' rule in South Carolina had been storm-tossed from the start, but its elimination in favor of crown authority after an uprising of 1719 touched off by a series of wildly arbitrary executive decrees and disallowances, did not end the colony's factionalism. Within a decade of the arrival of the first royal governor the opposition in the Commons House, invulnerable to administrative pressure and driven to extremities by a sudden collapse of the naval stores market, clashed so savagely with the governor and Council that the most elementary functions of government could not be continued: the provincial government simply ceased to exist, and remained inoperative for over two years while the public life of the colony dissolved into chaos. Order was gradually restored in the course of the following decade, but until the arrival of Governor Glen in 1743 the age-old rhythm of the colony's politics—"a period of violent internal

[7] Robert Proud, *The History of Pennsylvania, in North America* . . . (Philadelphia, 1797–98), II, 44; Carl Bridenbaugh, ed., *Gentleman's Progress: The Itinerarium of Dr. Alexander Hamilton, 1744* (Chapel Hill, 1948), p. 29; Frederick B. Tolles, *Meeting House and Counting House: The Quaker Merchants of Colonial Philadelphia, 1682–1763* (Chapel Hill, 1948), p. 17; J. R. Pole, *Political Representation in England and the Origins of the American Republic* (London, 1966), p. 118; Theodore Thayer, "The Quaker Party of Pennsylvania, 1755–1765," *Pennsylvania Magazine of History and Biography,* 71 (1947), 19–43. Pole's survey of Pennsylvania's politics (pp. 76–124) is particularly useful in its emphasis on the Assembly leaders' fears of a threatened extension of proprietary patronage, and on the existence on both sides of suspicions that efforts were being made to destroy the balance of the constitution: "The publications of the Assembly constantly laid stress on the sinister designs of the Governor and his creatures, but it is at least worth noting that, from the standpoint of the proprietors, the designs of the Assembly might seem equally sinister, equally tending to the subversion of the legitimate balance of power" (p. 114).

dispute resulting in near anarchy followed by a period of adjustment and relaxation of tensions"—continued. A sustained equilibrium was reached during the twelve and a half years of Glen's administration, but only because that weak and feckless executive, "pathetically eager . . . to please" and totally bereft of influence in a House elected triennially by secret ballot on universal white suffrage—an executive, moreover, relieved by an independent salary from the necessity of imposing himself on the legislature—refused to assert the powers of his office. When Glen in desperation in 1748 vetoed two bills and prorogued the House against its will, his actions were instantly disowned by the Council and publicly denounced as portentous throwbacks to Stuart autocracy. The *South Carolina Gazette* lectured him vigorously on the evils of naked prerogative, and treated him to extended instruction on good and evil magistrates and on the capacity of the people to govern themselves. When the Board of Trade after 1748 insisted that he play his full role in government, he found himself pitched into controversy with the House equipped only with the negative weapons of veto and prorogation, and his authority dissolved with scarcely a tremor. It was left to his more ambitious successors to attempt to discipline by sheer prerogative a Commons House they could not politically control.[8]

North Carolina's royal government emerged from even more chaotic origins than South Carolina's. When after the collapse of the Proprietary government the first royal governor, George Burrington, a wild-tempered, foul-mouthed martinet, attempted by fiat to force from the primitive legislature a minimum of obedience to crown instructions, the opposition in both Council and House, not satisfied with fighting him to a standstill, plotted to assassinate him. His two successors, Gabriel Johnston

---

[8] M. Eugene Sirmans, *Colonial South Carolina, a Political History 1663–1763* (Chapel Hill, 1966), pp. 223, 235, and chaps. x–xii generally; for the importance of Glen's lack of patronage powers, see especially p. 234.

(1734–1752) and Arthur Dobbs (1754–1765), served in a more tranquil age; each was more effective than his predecessor. But while Johnston managed to establish a more or less viable government, the only way he could control the worst of the opposition was either by repeatedly proroguing and dissolving the Assembly or by convening it at times and places that guaranteed the absence of the most difficult members, a maneuver that led in the end to the destruction of government's authority altogether in the northern half of the colony. Dobbs was more sophisticated and his stake in the colony's economic fortunes was deeper, but though successful in many of his efforts, he found it impossible to come to terms with an opposition "junto" that harassed him and tied up his government at every turn: this intractable band of "self-interested gentlemen" caucused secretly, he believed, for the purpose of using their control of the Assembly to destroy him and the authority he represented.[9]

Maryland, one might have thought, held out the best prospect of an integrated, disciplined, and effective government in eighteenth-century terms, for the Proprietary family was not only responsible, active, and thoroughly involved in the colony's affairs, but it commanded patronage in church and state worth an estimated £32,500 a year. Yet "at no time in the eighteenth century, from the restoration of proprietary government [1715] to the Revolution, was there even an interval of real political peace in Maryland." Proprietary power, it was found in Maryland, was prerogative power in its most extreme and obnoxious form: a land policy that was quasi-feudal, an executive jurisdiction that was "Stuarchal," and a cluster of social and economic privileges that seemed arbitrary and unnatural. The House of

---

[9] Dobbs's conflicts with "the junto" are documented throughout volumes V and VI of William L. Saunders, ed., *The Colonial Records of North Carolina* (Raleigh, N. C., 1886–90), e.g., VI, 319 ff.; the general history of factionalism in North Carolina is ably summarized under various headings in Jack P. Greene, *The Quest for Power* (Chapel Hill, 1963).

Delegates' reactions to the use of such power ran to extremes. Its Place Acts barred officeholders from sitting in the House and thus helped nullify the legislative power of patronage. In resolutions and petitions to the crown the House declared illegal all fees, taxes, and duties not enacted by the Assembly; condemned the buying and selling of offices; demanded agency representation in England; and claimed all the rights and privileges of the House of Commons. On these issues Court and Country deadlocked as early as 1739 (the struggle had begun in the twenties), and they remained deadlocked through periods of active combat and passive hostility until in the early 1760's the claims and counterclaims of these irreconcilable antagonists merged into those of a greater controversy.[10]

In some of the colonies, at certain times, accommodations were reached and calm prevailed. But when that happened for any length of time—when "there was nothing to do but to govern"—it was in almost every case the result of a governor's refusal to exercise the power of his office, for, as Governor Shirley told the Duke of Newcastle in 1750, "in every govern-

---

[10] Charles A. Barker, *The Background of the Revolution in Maryland* (New Haven, 1940), pp. 151, 214, 230 ff., and chap. vii generally. Cf. Donnell M. Owings, *His Lordship's Patronage: Offices of Profit in Colonial Maryland* (Baltimore, 1953).

[11] Charles H. Lincoln, ed., *Correspondence of William Shirley . . . 1731–1760* (New York, 1912), I, 494. "The colony [Virginia] found political peace in the personage of Major Hugh Drysdale, a mild-mannered administrator whose every action was prefaced by a desire to avoid trouble. A governor who did not cause trouble was one who did not seek to limit colonial prerogatives, insist rigidly upon royal authority, meddle in religious affairs, or try to reform Virginian customs and institutions. He was an Edward Nott, a Hugh Drysdale, or a William Gooch." David A. Williams, "Political Alignments in Colonial Virginia Politics, 1698–1750" (unpubl. diss., Northwestern Univ., 1959), p. 210. For Gooch's willingness to serve as a "spokesman for the legislature," see also Osgood, *American Colonies in the Eighteenth Century*, IV, chap. vii.

ment where His Majesty's governor is active in doing his duty" there will be "secret practices or open clamors of particular malignant persons . . . no providence can prevent 'em." So, in these terms, there was harmony in **Virginia** during Drysdale's and much of Gooch's administrations (1722–49), a placid interval between the tumultuous factionalism of the Howard-Andros-Nicholson-Spotswood era and the uproar of the Pistole Free controversy.[11] The basic pattern remained that of conflict—conflict shaped by the incompatibility between, on the one hand, a legally swollen but politically shrunken prerogative, and on the other hand, a "democracy" that was easily capable of resisting "influence" and that was continuously stimulated to action by shifts in the mobile economy and society and by arbitrary movements of patronage politics in England.

There was, however, one striking exception, the result neither of executive inertia nor of peculiar characteristics of governmental organization, but rather of a fortuitous conjunction of economic and political forces that made possible the construction of a single, tightly integrated hierarchy of authority. This exception was **New Hampshire**, during the twenty-five-year governorship of Benning Wentworth (1741–66). For though Wentworth too, in the early years of his administration, clashed savagely with his House of Representatives, in the end he found himself in possession of power so great and so necessary to the welfare of the colonists that he was able to obliterate political opposition. New Hampshire was a single-industry colony. Its economy was altogether dependent on the timber and naval stores trade, and this trade in turn was heavily dependent—in law entirely dependent, for certain categories of goods—on the huge market created by the British navy. Through Wentworth's years this market was largely controlled by John Thomlinson, who was closely associated with both the ministry and powerful Whig merchants, and was also deputy paymaster of His Majesty's troops in America and the official agent of the colony of New Hampshire in London. This strategically placed and influential politician and commercial operator was able to assign to Wentworth powers of contract and purchase, of credit and payment, which, together with the monopoly of land grants and the gifts of local office that Wentworth controlled through his governorship, "made Wentworth's management of provincial political institutions a relatively easy task." He packed the Council with his supporters, intervened successfully in local elections, bought the favor of the representatives he did not select, and filled the local offices—"judges and justices . . . the secretary, treasurer, sheriff, register of probate, and the military officers" —with his own men. When in 1748 the one serious challenge to Wentworth's rule was launched, simultaneous calls on reserves of "interest" in London and New Hampshire put it down so effectively that the administration was stronger after the flare-up than it had been before.[12]

****

New Hampshire under Benning Wentworth—politically tranquil not, like Virginia under Gooch, as a result of the powerlessness and inertia of the executive but of the fortuitous accumulation and the energetic disposal of "influence" in extraordinary quantities—New Hampshire is the exception that helps explain the rule. For the history of politics in eighteenth-century America is the history of factionalism born of a political system anomalous in its essence, lacking in what any objective observer would consider a minimal degree of functional integration. But participants in eighteenth-century politics, and

[12] Jere R. Daniell, "Politics in New Hampshire under Governor Benning Wentworth, 1741–1767," *William and Mary Quarterly*, 3rd ser., 23 (1966), 76–105; the quotations are on pp. 91, 89.

contemporary interpreters of it, were not wholly objective, they were certainly not neutral, observers. They viewed the political world around them through the perceptual apparatus of eighteenth-century Britons—through the system of ideas that had evolved around the concept of mixed government and had reached its fullest elaboration at the hands of the "country" opposition under Walpole. It is in the meaning this rampant factionalism acquired in minds steeped in the literature of eighteenth-century British politics that the deeper historical significance of colonial politics may be seen to lie.

The efforts that were made in the colonies to comprehend and explain this political system within the commonly accepted categories of thought were strenuous; at times they seem to have been almost desperate. Frequently as one reads through the pamphlet and newspaper polemics that accompanied the factional battles, one has the sense that the sheer explosiveness of the controversies are propelling men's minds beyond the frontiers of eighteenth-century political culture, toward a mode of understanding altogether new, altogether modern.

Parties and factions—their destructiveness, the history of the evils they brought upon mankind, their significance as symptoms of disease in the body politic —are endlessly discussed in the public prints; they are endlessly condemned and endlessly abjured. But then, suddenly, a new note is struck. At the height of the Morris-Cosby struggle of the early 1730's a column appeared in the *New York Gazette* that began with the usual encomium to the "even balance of authority resulting from the mutual dependence of [the] several parts" of the English constitution, "the most complete and regular [constitution] that has ever been contrived by the wisdom of man"—all this the most routine sentiment. Then suddenly the thought shifts.

A free government [the writer states] cannot but be subject to *parties, cabals,* and *intrigues.* This perhaps may be formed into an objection against free governments by the advocates for absolute power, but for that reason it is of no weight. I have somewhere seen opposition of interests called a curse attending free governments because it is inseparable from them. When it tends to *sap the foundations of the constitution* then indeed it properly deserves that name, but to pronounce the opposition of those a curse who from a just zeal and jealousy for their liberty endeavor to defeat schemes of power destructive of liberty is the dialect and language of tools of power and sycophants. I may venture to say that some opposition, though it proceed not entirely from a public spirit, is not only necessary in free governments but of great service to the public. Parties are a check upon one another, and by keeping the ambition of one another within bounds, serve to maintain the public liberty. Opposition is the life and soul of public zeal which, without it, would flag and decay for want of an opportunity to exert itself . . . It may indeed proceed from wrong motives, but still it is necessary . . . Nor have [the administration] any reason to repine at it or to wish it at an end since whatever motives it may have proceeded from, it has proved of service both to them and to the public, even contrary perhaps to the *design and intent of the authors of it.*[13]

13 *New York Gazette,* March 11–18, 1733/34.

The date is 1733: well before the time such views would gain even incidental recognition in England.[14] The statement was immediately challenged in the next issue of the *Gazette* and the argument drawn back to conventional ground from its advance toward an interest-group theory of politics—a theory that would, half a century later, be freshly propounded by James Madison and enshrined, to the edification of the twentieth century, in the tenth *Federalist* paper. So the thought trailed away. But it recurs—here and there in the colonies, as men sought to comprehend the actuality of politics they saw about them. Five years later a Pennsylvania writer declared "there can be no liberty without faction, for the latter cannot be suppressed without introducing slavery in the place of the former." Ten years after that a contributor to *The New York Gazette Revived in the Weekly Post-Boy*, concerned not with Cosby but with Clinton, announced that

> regard for liberty has always made me think that parties in a free state ought rather to be considered as an advantage to the public than an evil. Because while they subsist I have viewed them as so many spies upon one another, ready to proclaim abroad and warn the public of any attack or encroachment upon the public liberty and thereby rouse the members thereof to assert those rights they are [entitled?] to by the laws.

[14] Thus almost none of the examples of the advocacy of party before Burke that Caroline Robbins has uncovered are dated before 1733; none are as pointed or direct as the statement of the *Gazette*. Caroline Robbins, " 'Discordant Parties,' A Study of the Acceptance of Party by Englishmen," *Political Science Quarterly*, 73 (1958), 520 ff.

Once again the thought trails away; but again it reveals an effort to go beyond the standard formulations to a new paradigm altogether, to a mode of thought that is fresher, closer to the grain of reality.[15]

The same impulse takes other expressions. William Livingston's *Independent Reflector,* though it is for the most part a compendium of the standard formulas of eighteenth-century political thought, contains in a few sections propositions altogether modern, far in advance of anything one might expect to have emerged from the mid-eighteenth century and from a society that venerated the concept of the monarchy. What Livingston was in effect saying in his six essays on the proposed Anglican college is not simply that an institution supported by public funds should be nonsectarian: that students be permitted to worship in any mode they choose and that the official prayers of the college be reduced to the least offensive common denominator; nor is it simply that the control of the institution should be vested in the hands of Assembly-picked trustees, on the grounds that the Assembly was "split into so great a variety of opinions and professions [that] . . . the jealousy of all parties combating each other would inevitably produce a perfect freedom for each particular party." Beyond all of this, what Livingston was saying was that the crown—that is, the interest of the state in its highest, most abstract and symbolic form—was itself factious; that there was no im-

<hr>

[15] *Pennsylvania Gazette,* March 21–30, 1737/38; *New York Gazette Revived in the Weekly Post-Boy,* Jan. 9, 1748/49. Cf. *"View of* Parties *and* Opposition," in *New York Gazette,* March 11–18, 1734/35.

partial interest of the state that stood above the conflicts of ordinary interests; that the state itself did not exist other than as a faction or party involved like any other faction or party in the everyday competition for power. Do not accept a crown charter, Livingston explained, for "it is not only the King's prerogative to grant a charter but also to grant it upon certain terms"—terms favorable not to the public at large but to "one particular party." The public and private happiness of the province is advanced, he said, not by the presumed impartiality of the crown but only by the immediate legislative body in which every move "tending to abridge the liberty of any particular sect would by some or other of our representatives be strongly opposed"—an extraordinary consideration, in the eighteenth century, this emphatic assertion that the crown, the embodiment of the state, was itself factious.[16] Yet it was no more than a lucid perception that penetrated through the veils of conventional thought to the flesh of actuality. In 1701 orders had gone out from London to all governors forbidding them to join in any faction or party, insisting that they represent the crown as above

[16] William Livingston, *et al.*, *The Independent Reflector*, ed. Milton M. Klein (Cambridge, Mass., 1963), pp. 201–202, 195, 197, 196. The six essays are nos. 17–22. The *New York Mercury*'s revealing response to what it called the *Reflector*'s "republican scheme for the government of your college" appeared in the issue of July 30, 1753. The *Mercury* argued that the government of the college should reflect the government of the nation—in both constitutions, power should be "partly in the crown and partly in the people"—and that under the *Reflector*'s scheme "upon the death of every trustee the whole province may be put in a ferment, and room be left for a certain restless enterprising sect to worm themselves gradually into the sole government of it."

such partisan contentions, the assumption persisting that "it is a fundamental maxim in politics, that the *government ought to be of no party at all.*" But in 1752 Archibald Kennedy, in his *Essay on the Government of the Colonies,* expressed the universal experience, to which Livingston was responding, when he wrote: "A governor is no sooner appointed than the first question is, Into whose hands shall I throw myself? The answer is ready, Into whose but such as can best manage the Assembly. Hence prime ministers and courtiers are established, and, of course, anti-courtiers."[17]

Such forays beyond the boundaries of accepted thought are of course uncommon (though traces of them may be found in the literature of almost every colony). Yet when they do appear (as in the case of the most famous of them, the Morrisite insistence in the Zenger trial that despite the clarity of the law to the contrary, truth *should* be an acceptable defense against the charge of seditious libel) they are impressive and provoking.

[17] Leonard W. Labaree, ed., *Royal Instructions to British Colonial Governors, 1670–1776* (New York and London, 1935), I, 84; *New England Courant,* Nov. 13–20, 1721; [Archibald Kennedy], *An Essay on the Government of the Colonies* (New York, 1752), p. 34. Kennedy continues: ". . . hence parties are formed, and thus the peace of the public is destroyed, honest neighbors set together by the ears, and all good fellowship excluded the society; elections are carried on with great animosity and at a vast expense, as if our alls were at stake. And what is all this for? Is the public good really the point in view? Or is it to show how dexterously the one side can manage the Assembly for [the governor] and the other side against him? Let us be told what mighty advantage the public has reaped from that repeated round of squabbles we have been pestered with, with no other view than to distress a worthy gentleman."

They foreshadow the future; they point to the direction the generality of thought would one day take. But most often the boundaries are not crossed. The typical responses to the politics of the day flow from within the commonplaces of eighteenth-century English thought, which take on, in the context of American politics, a heightened, a portentous meaning.

Their intellectual world framed by the concept of the mixed constitution, the colonists found ready at hand, in the terms of that powerful paradigm, a means of comprehending the disturbances around them. Some, reflecting on the socio-constitutional structure of colonial society, were struck by the discrepancies between the ideal and the real, the English model and the colonial duplicates, and attributed their ills to these discrepancies. It was often noted that the all-important middle order, the element of aristocracy—so vital, according to the standard constitutional theory, in keeping the extremes of power and liberty from tearing each other apart—was not properly represented in the colonies, in certain cases did not exist at all. When from time to time the Assemblies were lectured by the governors, as was New York's by Governor Fletcher in 1693, that "you ought to let the Council have a share [in the government]; they are in the nature of the House of Lords, or upper house; but you seem to take the whole power in your hands, and set up for every thing," the opposition replied, in Cadwallader Colden's words, that "the most opulent families, in our own memory, have risen from the lowest ranks of people" and hence one could scarcely say that there was a traditional aristocracy in social terms, and further, that there was no demarcation in legal status between those who were officially members of the middle order and those who were not. The authority of the councillors, it was said in New York in 1711, flows not "from their being another distinct state or rank of people in the constitution, which they are not, being all commons, but only from the mere pleasure of the prince," with the result that the middle order in the colonies, by this definition, lacked the independence that was its chief constitutional virtue in England.[18]

At times this definition of the problem of the middle order itself stood at the heart of bitter factional fighting. So in Pennsylvania the long struggle culminating in the mid-1720's between the forces of James Logan and those of David Lloyd and William Keith came to center on the validity of the analogy of the Pennsylvania Council to England's House of Lords, Logan arguing that from England's "happy constitution . . . [are] the governments of the King's plantations . . . modelled, for in them the Council board is appointed to bear the same resemblance both to the House of Lords and Privy Council that the Assembly does to the House of Commons," Lloyd replying that the constitution of Pennsylvania derived only from Penn's Frame of 1701, which denied veto power to the Council. In Maryland, too, it was said contentiously

---

[18] Smith, *History of the Late Province of New York,* I, 115; E. B. O'Callaghan and Berthold Fernow, eds., *Documents Relative to the Colonial History of the State of New York . . .* (Albany, 1856–87), VII, 705; *Journal of the Legislative Council of the Colony of New-York [1691–1755] . . .* (Albany, 1861), I, 329.

that "the Upper House is no part of our constitution"; "we know nothing," the Maryland House declared, of "the rights and privileges of those gentlemen that are said to constitute another branch." And in South Carolina, in an elaborate debate on the way in which that colony's government might most closely be made to approximate the balance of the English government, it was stressed by the opposition that "the scheme formed by the late Lords Proprietors for making a nobility in this province to represent an upper house" had failed; "since there is no nobility, . . . [and] one estate or part of the British constitution being wanted," to allow an appointed Council serving *"durante bene placito regis"* to act as if it were a true House of Lords "must necessarily destroy the balance and be contrary to the usage of our mother country." To press the analogy of the Council and the Lords was in the end absurd: "The Lords are independent and not to be displaced at pleasure of a minister . . . The councillors in Carolina are dependent and hold their places during pleasure. The councillors in Carolina vote for members of Assembly, and have their representatives. Can they represent themselves and be represented? . . . Can a peer of England be suspended?"[19]

[19] *Pennsylvania Archives*, 8th ser., II, 1638, 1686–87 (cf. Roy N. Lokken, *David Lloyd*, Seattle, 1959, chap. xxi); Evarts B. Greene *The Provincial Governor in the English Colonies of North America* (Cambridge, Mass., 1898), p. 88; *Supplement to the South Carolina Gazette*, May 13, 1756. For further discussion of the relative power, in comparison with that of the equivalent parts of the English constitution, of the Commons House and the Council in South Carolina, see *South Carolina Gazette*, May 6, 22, 29, and especially the seven-page issue of June 5, 1756.

Deviations from England's mixed constitution were in other ways noted and in other ways involved in the controversies of the time. William Smith, surveying the whole of New York's experience with gubernatorial salaries, declared that "the particular state of this province differs so widely from that of their mother country that we ought not in this respect to follow the custom of the Commons. Our constitution, as some observe, is so imperfect, in numberless instances, that the rights of the people lie, even now, at the mere mercy of their governors; and granting a perpetual support, it is thought, would be in reality little less than the loss of everything dear to them." The Massachusetts House twenty years earlier had said the same thing in different, subtler words when explaining the colony's constitution to the harassed William Burnet. The House agreed that Massachusetts' constitution was a replica of England's; but it was "the peculiar distinction and glory of the British constitution that every part of it had a mutual relation to and dependence on each other according to the different powers or privileges respectively belonging to each," which, they said, was precisely why, given the Council's dependence on the governor "for their very being" and given the variety of other unusual powers of the executive in the colony, the House had resolved never to settle a permanent salary on the governors. Similarly in Pennsylvania in 1738 admirers of England's mixed constitution condemned as absurd the claim "that the government of this province is defective as far as it wants an exact resemblance to that of our mother country." The original circumstances in the two cases had been altogether different: "the three estates of King, Lords, and Commons took their rise not from any deep previous thought or original contrivance but from the manner and circumstances in which the Saxons first took possession of England," but the Pennsylvania constitution was devised by those who "had seen and felt the effects of *DESPOTISM at home*" and who therefore deliberately lodged "the *WHOLE* legislative power . . . where it is always safest lodged, *in the hands of the people*." "To cry up the necessity of reducing the form of this government to the British model," consequently, was "a design almost as wicked as was the attempt to change the English *constitution* into a *democracy*," steps in that direction "throwing a greater share of power into the governor's hands than is consistent with our liberties."[20]

Yet, though at certain times and in certain ways in the heat of factional controversy elements in the colonial

[20] Smith, *History of the Late Province of New-York*, I, 308–309; *Journals of the House of Representatives of Massachusetts, 1727–1729* (Boston, 1927), pp. 279, 280; *Pennsylvania Gazette*, March 21–30, 1737/38. The historical origins of the three constituent elements of the British constitution, according to the *Gazette*, lay in the Saxon conquest of England, the invaders dividing up the land "each man a share according to his merit and post in the military expedition . . . The general was the first estate, the officers the second, and the soldiers in their collective bodies made up the third." For the revealing debate in Maryland, which anticipated the pivotal problem of constitutionalism in the Revolutionary period, of "whether a Parliament (or in America, an Assembly, for I presume none will pretend to make any material distinction) has a power, *i.e.* a right, to enact anything contrary to a fundamental part of the British constitution," see *Maryland Gazette*, Feb. 10, April 20, 27, May 4, 11, and *Postscript* to issue 1748.

constitutions were found imperfect in comparison with the parental model, and the proportions and emphasis of the whole were seen to be rather different, the ideal, setting the terms of reference for all constitutional and political discussions, remained England's mixed constitution. It was by the essential similarities presumed to exist between the model and its colonial derivatives, and not by the differences, that the most fundamental responses to colonial politics were formed. For English constitutional theory of the eighteenth century, especially as developed by the opposition groups under Walpole, offered, within its own distinctive categories, a mode of comprehension of such an inflamed, anomalous politics; and it is this mode of understanding—flowing directly from the main sources of the colonists' political culture and serving so aptly to explain the excesses of the politics around them —that forms the background of the American Revolution.

What the colonial opposition at every stage saw in contemplating the role of government, of power, of the executive, in the colonies were evidences—scattered to be sure, fading in and out of focus, rising and falling in importance, but palpable evidences nevertheless—of "Robinarchal" conspiracy against the constitutional guarantees of liberty. The presence of a Fletcher, of a Cornbury, or even of such benign and ineffective men as Shute and Clinton, Glen and Johnston, evoked the cluster of ideas and images associated with arbitrary power, the drives of ambition, and the innocent-seeming origins of despotism. That governors "*can do* and have *with im-*

punity done many injuries is but too evident to be denied," Zenger's *Journal* declared in 1734. "A governor turns rogue, does a thousand things for which a small rogue would have deserved a halter," and is joined in his roguery by wretches too avaricious or too cowardly to stand up to him. Though this is "an age of liberty in which *the slavish doctrine of passive obedience* is out of fashion," the *Journal* continued,

> There have been *Nicholsons, Cornburys, Cootes, Burringtons, Edens, Lowthers, Georges, Parkes, Douglases* and many more, as very bashaws as ever were sent from Constantinople; and there have not been wanting under each of their administrations, persons the dregs and scandal of humane nature *who have kept in with them,* and used their endeavors to enslave their fellow subjects, and persuaded others to do so too . . . an ill governor not only enslaves the present generation, but makes slavery hereditary to latest posterity . . .[21]

[21] *New York Weekly Journal,* Jan. 21, 1733[/34]. The fact that the word "governor" was commonly used in the English opposition literature to refer generically to rulers, especially despotic rulers, facilitated the application of that literature to immediate colonial problems. Often the colonists played on the word to heighten the innuendo. E.g., the *South Carolina Gazette,* in the course of republishing, for the most part without attribution, a series of papers from *Cato's Letters* (some, apparently, taken at third hand from the Boston *Independent Advertiser*), allowed that "it is evident from history that GOVERNORS have commonly been the aggressors, and led the way to *public confusions* . . . There is something so bewitching in power that we cannot wonder to see *governors* using all their endeavors to extend it . . . As I was dipping this morning into a book that lay before me, I was furnished with the following remarks: 'When we hear any sort of men complain, as some sort of men do frequently complain, that *governors* want power, we should ask them whether they mean over themselves . . . The truth is, they who complain thus do only want

The atmosphere created by such men was heavy with portents of "plots and conspiracies"—just such "rebellions, plots, and conspiracies," the *New England Courant* explained to its readers in a long essay of 1723, as "have been hatched, carried on, and supported by those who have been the greatest sticklers for [the] doctrines . . . of *passive obedience* and *nonresistance*," namely, Popish princes, Stuart despots, and the power-mad satraps of the East. Often ministerial—gubernatorial—engrossers of power have concerted their "SCHEMES OF GENERAL OPPRESSION AND PILLAGE, SCHEMES TO DEPRECIATE OR EVADE THE LAWS, RESTRAINTS UPON LIBERTY AND PROJECTS FOR ARBITRARY WILL" at the behest of their superiors, being mere instruments "of *Caesar* and *Augustus*"—instruments, Zenger explained, which at times have been used only to be discarded as sacrifices "to the pleasure and revenge of the people. Thus *Caesar Borgia* used *Ramiro D'Orco*, Governor of Ramagna . . . to commit cruelties, [and] then executed [him] for having committed them. Thus were EMPSON and DUDLEY used, and thus the great Turk often uses his bashaws."[22] This was not the likely case in the British world, however, for the motives of the English King were

---

to increase the *power of governors* because by it *their own* would be increased, and other advantages acquired.' . . . I have hitherto spoken of *governors* in general, without distinguishing between them and their *agents*, otherwise commonly called *ministers* . . ." *South Carolina Gazette*, July 29–August 1, 1748. (Italics in original.)

[22] *New England Courant*, June 17–24, 1723; *New York Weekly Journal*, Jan. 28, 1733[/34].

not to be questioned. The King, it was universally agreed, would do no wrong; but his ministers and other underlings often had and no doubt would again.[23] Chieftains sent to the colonies were known to have used the age-old first step of deceiving the King, hiding from him the complaints of the people in order to advance their selfish ends. To a Virginia essayist of 1701 (most probably William Byrd II) this was the "greatest unhappiness the plantations labor under, . . . that the King and court of England are altogether strangers to the true state of affairs in America . . . that is the true cause why their grievances have not been long since redressed."[24] Ministerial dissimulation, once it had begun, could scarcely be controlled. Clothing themselves in an aura of true patriotism carefully calculated to deceive the naive and incautious—professing to be self-sacrificing students of the general good—power-hungry governors, like power-hungry ministers throughout history, could be understood to be elaborating schemes of deliberate corruption which would end in the destruction of the balance of the constitution and an executive engrossment of power.

There was, consequently, no more important political problem, nor one more commonly and elaborately discussed in the public prints in the colonies, than that of distinguishing true from dissembling patriots. Essay after

[23] For a characteristic application of this commonplace idea, referring to the claim of the Parliament of 1641 that it "made war against the King for the King's service," see *Pennsylvania Gazette,* April 1–8, 22–29, 1736.

[24] Louis B. Wright, ed., *An Essay Upon the Government of the English Plantations on the Continent of America (1701)* (San Marino, Calif., 1945), p. 37.

essay appeared on the subject in the newspapers (some of them original essays, some properly attributed reprints of English essays, some wholesale plagiarisms); pamphlet after pamphlet discoursed on the subject; speeches and letters dilated on it. The problem was full of difficulties. "Some princes," *The Boston Evening Post* quoted from an English periodical, "who have aimed at despotic power . . . have, even in their own dominions, been at the bottom of insurrections themselves and set their creatures underhand to stir up and encourage their subjects to revolt" against themselves knowing they could easily subdue them and force them to purchase their lives with their liberties. The strategies of pseudo-patriots possessed by "that monster, *the lust of lawless authority*" were manifold and subtle, the *Pennsylvania Journal* explained in 1758 in an elaborate series of essays by "The Watchman" devoted to revealing the "artifices by which the villains of the political world, both small and great, generally mislead the easy multitude who entrust them with power." Quoting Bolingbroke's "elegant expressions" to the effect that there never can be a time when "liberty is entirely free from immediate or remote danger"; citing the examples of Pisistratus subverting the government of Athens "and enslaving that wise and brave people while they thought he was protecting them," and of Julius Caesar courting popularity so successfully that "Rome gave him an army and that army gave him . . . Rome," "The Watchman" laid out the inner workings of conspiracy against the public good."[25]

[25] *Boston Evening Post*, May 19, 1755, quoting "*The* HU-MOURIST. *Of* PATRIOTISM," explaining how "those who would attempt the subversion of a government . . . disguise

There were degrees of villainy to be noted, "The Watchman" pointed out, and variations in the patterns of "design." There have been, first, "traitors of the first magnitude"—bold, self-confident, domineering: "those

their designs under a show of public spirit and zeal for the liberties of their country." *Pennsylvania Journal and Weekly Advertiser,* Aug. 17, 1758.

The eight "Watchman" essays, initially directed against the dominance of the Quaker oligarchy in the Pennsylvania Assembly, together constitute an exhaustive analysis of the nature of political conspiracy, and anticipate in detail the critical discussion of "design" that took place during the Revolutionary years. Seven of the eight essays (which were explicitly based on—many passages were taken verbatim from—*Cato's Letters,* Bolingbroke, Sidney, and the Whig historians Rapin, Burnet, Ralph, and White Kennett) appeared in the *Journal* (issues of Feb. 23, March 16, 30, April 27, May 11, Aug. 3, 17, 1758); the eighth essay appeared only in William Bradford's *The American Magazine, and Monthly Chronicle for the British Colonies,* issue of August, 1758. *The American Magazine,* which was sponsored by the same group that supported the *Journal* and was edited by Provost William Smith of the College of Philadelphia, republished four of the other papers in that series. (Lyon N. Richardson, *A History of Early American Magazines, 1741–1789,* New York, 1931, pp. 106–107.) The elaborate replies to "The Watchman," to which the young Joseph Galloway was the main contributor (they continued his long-standing polemic with William Smith), and the other ideological pieces stimulated by the series, dwell with particular emphasis on the history of the plots and counterplots of the 1680's and on the history of Parliament from Charles II to George II. These replies, and "The Watchman" essays themselves, served to bring the ideological issues and the heated political atmosphere of the 1680's directly and fully into the awareness of Americans of the late 1750's and to relate them to the problems of American politics. See especially the *Journal* issues of March 9, 23, April 13, 20, Sept. 28, and Oct. 5, 1758; and Galloway's *A True and Impartial State of the Province of Pennsylvania . . .* (Philadelphia, 1759), replying to Smith's *A Brief State of the Province of Pennsylvania . . .* (London, 1755), and to his *A Brief View of the Conduct of Pennsylvania . . .* (London, 1756). Cf. Bernard Bailyn, *The Ideological Origins of the American Revolution* (Cambridge, 1967), chap. iv.

daring spirits who seem intended as the scourges of the human race. Their whole aim is glory and despotic sway." They characteristically "preserve the appearance of the most submissive servants *only* until they know they are masters"; then once "the building was complete, they kicked down the useless scaffolding . . . defied the resentment of an injured people, and smiled at their own iniquities when they knew them[selves] above punishment." More common and more immediate were the threats that came not from these master figures but from "*traitors minorum gentium* . . . They do not fly at such great game as the destruction of nations. They are not eagles in prey but a kind of low animals, raven-like feeding upon carrion or filth about the ditches and hedges. Avarice is their idol, and they are content if they can heap its shrine with a few stolen spoils picked up from the blotches and sores of their country . . . They endeavor to make up in craft . . . these *lefthanded Walsinghams* . . . what they want in spirit and conduct." But both—conspirators great and conspirators small—use as their major stratagem "pretended struggles for the rights of the people" which are "so advantageous a piece of craft to wicked leaders that if there should ever happen to be no attempt made on the people they govern, they *conjure* up something that looks like it, fall furiously upon it . . . and then dub themselves protectors of the people and heroes of patriotism." Deceit, therefore, was the chief weapon of public malefactors everywhere; everywhere corrupt leaders were devoted to the maxim "that they must cover wicked designs with specious pretences and that the surest way to gain their point is by seeming not to aim at it." But in "no constitution or form of government" were they so likely to be successful in this as in "the mixed; and of the mixed, none are so subject to them as those which consist of TWO *parts*." It was in Pennsylvania above all, consequently, and in the other mixed governments of British North America, that lovers of liberty must be most alert to the signs of demagoguery.[26]

Formulas were suggested, tests outlined, by which true patriots could be distinguished from conspiratorial dissemblers. Patriots never seek office; they have it thrust upon them, and pride themselves in boasting, as did Franklin charged by "Proprietary minions and creatures" of having stirred up "uneasiness and distractions," that "in none of the fourteen elections you mention did I ever appear as a candidate. I never did, directly or indirectly, solicit any man's vote."[27] They do not seek office because they do not need office; independent in wealth and opinion, they cannot be bought or meanly influenced. They are—palpably, transparently—lovers of virtue. The good magistrate, the colonists quoted from the passage in Sidney they found reprinted in *Cato's Letters* no. 37 (*"Character of a Good and of an Evil Magistrate, Quoted from Algernon Sidney, Esq."*) and which they copied again and again into the colonial

[26] *Pennsylvania Journal and Weekly Advertiser*, Aug. 17, Aug. 3, 1758.
[27] *Supplement to the Pennsylvania Journal. No. 1146*, Nov. 22, 1764. The point is generalized in Livingston, *Independent Reflector*, no. 32: e.g., "To ask a man for his vote is a confession in the candidate that he is suspicious of his own merit. 'Tis a proof of his apprehensions that the sense of the public is against him" (p. 281).

newspapers—the good magistrate "thinks it a great part of his duty, by precept and example, to educate the youth in a love of virtue and truth." The good magistrate seeks union and harmony in the public; he is never found stirring dissension. Only the demagogue, who "fancies he is not made for the people but the people for him; that he does not govern for them but for himself; that the people live only to increase his glory"—it is only the demagogue who stirs dissension. "He does not inquire what he may do for them but what he may draw from them: by this means he sets up an interest of profit, pleasure, or pomp in himself repugnant to the good of the public." He declares the active defense of justice to be "sedition and rebellion," and strives to "diminish that strength, virtue, power, and courage which he knows to be bent against him." He is fearful of the truth, and so "will always, by tricks, artifices, cavils, and all means possible, endeavor to establish falsehood and dishonesty, whilst other emissaries and instruments of iniquity, by corrupting the youth and such as can be brought to lewdness and debauchery, bring the people to such a pass that they may neither care nor dare to vindicate their rights."[28]

[28] "*From* CATO'S LETTERS. *Character of a Good and of an Evil Magistrate, Quoted from* Algernon Sidney, *Esq.*," *South Carolina Gazette*, July 25–29, 1748; cf. e.g., the Boston *Independent Advertiser*, May 16, 1748. For other examples of the vast literature on good and evil (especially dissimulating) magistrates, see, besides the New England election sermons, *The Independent Advertiser*, May 9, 1748; William Penn's letter to the freeholders of Pennsylvania, reprinted in *South Carolina Gazette*, Oct. 23–30, 1736 (cf. *ibid.*, Dec. 28–Jan. 6, 1748[/49]); *Pennsylvania Journal and Weekly Advertiser*, March 9 and

Inevitably, therefore, the would-be Robinarch deals
in corruption; he is naturally led to use the array of well-
known devices available to executives seeking to corrupt
"the democracy" in a mixed government. He multiplies
offices in order to increase his power to purchase votes
and hence to enlarge his "interest" beyond its natural
boundaries—"increasing the number of officers dependent on the crown," the *Boston Weekly News-Letter*
put it in 1757, "and thereby influencing elections and
destroying the liberties of the people."[29] He seeks to increase taxes: stamp taxes (which had been in effect in
England since 1670 and had been proposed for the colonies again and again in the eighteenth century); excise
taxes (such as Walpole had attempted to levy in Eng-

Sept. 28, 1758; *Boston Evening Post,* May 10, 1742, May 21,
1750, May 19, 1755; *Boston Gazette,* June 23, 1755, April 26,
1756; *New York Mercury,* March 3, 1755.

[29] *Boston Weekly News-Letter,* March 31, 1757. So, fifteen
years earlier, in words prophetic of the Revolutionary generation's condemnation of English corruption and praise of American innocence and purity, a Boston pamphleteer warned of
"too great a number of placemen and pensioners sitting in Parliament." Let the lesson apply at home: "Will not such a noble
public spirit fire us with an honest zeal in this part of the world
to look about us and inquire if there have been any such among
us who have been influenced by posts of honor and profit to
vote and act too much as men in power would have them?
And if there have been such, to prevent it as much as may be
for the future by choosing such men only as are least likely
to be influenced thereby? I esteem it a great happiness that we
have not a great many posts of profit among us, and wish we
may be always so happy on that account. For it often happens
in many parts of the world that some of the most worthless
men enjoy them, and it's likely such men, who will do any
dirty work that a man of virtue would be ashamed of, will
enjoy them." *Boston Evening Post,* May 10, 1742, reprinting
"a small pamphlet . . . published here, entitled, *A Letter to the
Freeholders and Other Inhabitants of This Province* . . ."

land in 1733 and which the Massachusetts General
Court in 1754 sought to impose in that colony until
defeated, amid a flurry of local republications of the anti-
Walpole tracts of 1733);[30] and land taxes or fees—pistole
fees, for example. He uses every instrument available
to extend the lives of pliant Assemblies and destroy the
tenure of stubborn ones so as to attain that "corruption
and servile dependency of our . . . representatives," a
New York pamphleteer explained in 1732, that would
spell the end of liberty.[31] Above all, he seeks to suppress
freedom of speech and of the press, for "FREEDOM OF
SPEECH," Zenger's lawyer James Alexander explained
in an essay on the subject some 8,500 words in length, "is
a *principal pillar* in a free government": when this support
is taken away, the constitution is dissolved and tyranny is
erected on its ruins.[32]

This—in all governments at all times—was probably
the surest sign of the demagogue at work. It was certainly
so in the case of republics and limited monarchies, for
these governments "derive their strength and vigor from a
popular examination into the actions of the magistrates

[30] Paul S. Boyer, "Borrowed Rhetoric: The Massachusetts
Excise Controversy of 1754," *William and Mary Quarterly,*
3rd ser., 21 (1964), 328–351.

[31] Alexander Campbell, *Maxima Libertatis Custodia* . . .
(New York, 1732).

[32] Alexander's exhaustive essay, part of the polemics that
followed the Zenger trial, first appeared in four successive issues
of Franklin's *Pennsylvania Gazette* (Nov. 10–17 ff., 1737) and
was reprinted twice in America within two months, and again in
London in 1741. It has been republished in its entirety, together
with the associated documents, by Stanley N. Katz, in Appendix
C of his edition of Alexander's *A Brief Narrative of the Case
and Trial of John Peter Zenger* . . . (Cambridge, Mass., 1963).

. . . An evil magistrate entrusted with a POWER to *punish words* is armed with a WEAPON the most *destructive* and *terrible*. Under pretense of pruning off the exuberant branches, he frequently destroys the tree." So Augustus, "under the specious pretext of preserving the characters of the *Romans* from defamation," passed a law equating libel with treason, which "established his tyranny, and for one mischief it prevented, ten thousand evils, horrible and tremendous, sprung up in the place . . . The construction of words being arbitrary and left to the decision of the judges, no man could write or open his mouth without being in danger of forfeiting his head." So too Henry VIII had his "supple judges" construe into libels "and sometimes extended to high treason . . . every light expression which happened to displease him," and turned into an instrument of suppression the infamous Court of Star Chamber by which in later times *"Empson* and *Dudley,* two voracious dogs of prey, . . . exercised the most merciless acts of oppression." So too Charles I, when he "had formed a design to lay aside Parliaments and subvert the constitution," forbade the people, Clarendon was quoted as saying, *"so much as to speak of Parliaments or so much as to mention that Parliaments were again to be called,"* and he prosecuted men "for words spoken in the House." Charles II similarly revealed his purpose. In "secret league with France to render himself absolute and enslave his subjects" but shrewd enough to conceal "his designs under a deep hyprocrisy," he appointed a licenser of the stage and press and encouraged him "to debase the minds of the people [by permitting] all the shocking circumstances of immodest *double entendres,* obscene description, and lewd representation" and to sanction all sneers at religion. The climax had come in that "pregnant instance of the danger that attends a law for punishing words," the judicial murder, under the savage James II, by "a packed jury" and a judge *"in furore,"* of the immortal Algernon Sidney, who was executed as a traitor for *"imagining the death of the King . . . even while that imagination remain[ed] covert in the mind."* Thus "the British *Brutus,* the warm, the steady friend of Liberty, who from a diffuse love to mankind left them that invaluable legacy, his immortal discourses on government, *was* for those very discourses, MURDERED by the hands of lawless power."

None of this was strange, unreal, or excessively rhetorical to minds steeped in the political literature of eighteenth-century England.[33] The rise of arbitrary power

---

[33] "The Watchman," summarizing in his final letter the lessons to be derived from the many historical examples "of human misery and political perfidy" he had cited, denied that he meant literally "that a *Caesar* is undermining the constitution by corruption or a *Pisistratus* betraying it with borrowed virtues. I don't mean that *laws* are to yield to *arms* or that an *arbitrary power* is to be erected on the ruins of *liberty.* These things," he added with heavy irony, "require some abilities and resolution, and therefore we may be safe." But though he did not expect these chilling historical episodes to be repeated with literal exactness in British America, he confidently challenged his readers to "cast your eyes on your own affairs and see if you can discover no resemblance between them and those instances I have mentioned." Nor would the future necessarily be better. So far the colonists had been fortunate in that they had only been "abused, cheated, and deceived by men who had just understanding and courage enough to abuse, cheat, and deceive a people who were willing to be so used." But there was reason to believe that "you may in some period feel

in the midst of deepening corruption was an only too
reasonable, a too familiar story, told a hundred times over
in the pages of Bolingbroke, Trenchard, Gordon, Molesworth, Rapin, and Sidney—a story reinforced in its reality
in the colonies in many ways: reinforced even by those
random dispatches from foreign capitals that filled out the
columns of the colonial newspapers, dispatches often
months, sometimes years, out of date and usually unre-
lated to each other yet together capable of conveying a
mood, an attitude toward if not a clear depiction of the
greater world beyond Britain. Polish peasants, with
matted hair and wooden shoes, their country overrun by
"Russian troops . . . now in full march," were being
crushed again; French parlements had once again been
turned aside, and in that land "poor half-starved devils are
daily at work to supply the luxuries of an infamous court
and to support armies kept on foot to oppress them";
rivers of blood still flowed in Turkey: ambassadors are
"strangled there by order of the Grand Signior"; in Persia
a Shah who "had slaughtered thousands without remorse"
was himself butchered by his own officers and his successor massacred by the nobility that elevated him;
"banditti" swarmed through Italy; tyrants triumphed in
Asia; and of those two once-brilliant centers of "virtue,
knowledge, and great men," Rome and Greece, the one

the misfortunes of which I have given examples" more directly.
Thus, fear both of the existing situation and of the future had
led him to draw out the dramatic examples of the past and
point to their applications: "I must *watch*, I must *alarm*, I must
cry aloud for your *political salvation*." *American Magazine*,
Aug., 1758 (p. 549 in the bound volume).

had been reduced to "a herd of pampered monks and a few starving lay inhabitants" while the other contained but "a few abject, contemptible slaves, kept under ignorance, chains, and vileness by the Turkish monarch."[34]

England, the colonists knew from all the sources of political culture available to them, was a beacon in a world of deepening gloom. "Some kingdoms within less than a century of years last past," James Logan explained to the Pennsylvania House in 1725, have "been changed from a state of greatest freedom into the most absolute and arbitrary government. *Britain* is now almost the only remaining kingdom that enjoys the ancient perfect state of liberty with which other countries were formerly blessed, till politic arts and the contrivances of men truly ambitious and designing subverted those liberties and betrayed the unhappy subjects into the power of one person whose absolute will became the only rule of his government and his pleasure the only standard of all their laws, and measure of their obedience."[35] England stood

[34] *Independent Advertiser*, April 18, Jan. 11, and Feb. 29, 1748; *Pennsylvania Gazette*, April 15–22, 1736, Nov. 10–17, 1737. The *Independent Advertiser's* essay of Feb. 29, 1748, is taken entirely and verbatim from *Cato's Letters*, no. 38; the *South Carolina Gazette* reprinted the same essay in its issue of Aug. 1–8.

[35] *Pennsylvania Archives*, 8th ser., II, 1638. Expressions of this belief, juxtaposed with despairing descriptions of the rest of the world, can be cited voluminously from any period in the eighteenth century. See, e.g., the long quotation from "a late writer in an address to the farmers of England," in "The Watchman," no. 5, originally published in the *Pennsylvania Journal and Weekly Advertiser*, May 11, 1758, and reprinted eleven days later in the *New York Mercury*: readers were invited to "cast your eyes with me a little over this globe to view the deplorable state of your fellow creatures in other coun-

almost completely alone in the Old World, sustained in its distinctive role, so far successfully, by the skillful rebalancing of its constitution in the settlement that had followed the Glorious Revolution. But that settlement had not extended, fully, to America. The phalanx of strong guarantees against the authoritarian power of the state was missing here, and the situation here, consequently, was peculiarly dangerous, peculiarly delicate, peculiarly

tries . . . In *Russia, Poland, Bohemia, Hungary,* and many parts of *Germany* . . . there is no such things as freeholders. The countrymen are all slaves to the gentlemen. They belong to the landlord . . . and are bought and sold with the land . . . If their lord is ill-tempered, passionate, or drunk, they are beat without mercy, nor dare they murmur, much less resist. For if a gentleman kills one of his boors, he is not punished, and if he kills one belonging to another gentleman, he pays only five pounds damages, as if it were for one of his beasts . . . In many parts of *Germany,* all about the limits of manors you may see posts set up with painted boards on them representing some a man hanged, others a man with his hand cut off, which are put up by way of warnings to show the punishments that attend killing the game. I might carry you to *Turkey* and other parts of *Asia* to show you the deplorable state of human nature in these countries, groaning under a race of monsters that disgrace their very shape, in a condition so completely miserable that all I have mentioned above is nothing compared to it . . . But how different is the case amongst us! We enjoy an *unprecarious property,* and every man may freely taste the fruits of his own labors *under his vine and under his fig tree, none making him afraid* . . . The King upon his throne cannot exact a single *farthing* of our estates but what we have first freely consented to pay by laws of our own making. We cannot be dragged out in violation of *justice* and *right* to wade in seas of blood for satiating the avarice or ambition of a haughty monarch. We need not fear *racks* nor *stripes* nor *bonds* nor *arbitrary imprisonments* from any authority whatsoever; or should such prevail for a time *above law,* yet while the constitution remains sound we may be sure the very act would soon destroy itself and terminate at length in the utter ruin of the projectors. 'Tis our happiness too that our *minds* are as *free* as our *bodies* . . ."

demanding of the powers of vigilance and resistance. *Obsta principiis*—"nip the shoots of arbitrary power in the bud"[36]—which would be the watchword of the American Revolution, was the watchword of the colonial tribunate in the earliest years of the eighteenth century. The phrase sprang naturally to the lips of politicians struggling with executive powers legally "so absolute," the essayist of 1701 wrote in words that would be echoed throughout the colonial period, "that it is almost impossible to lay any sort of restraint upon them."[37]

Yet if this regressive aspect of colonial politics conjured up in the minds of opposition, anti-gubernatorial groups in the colonies the elaborate image of ministerial conspiracy—of deliberate though dissembled efforts on the part of the first order of the constitution to destroy the balance of the constitution and engross the whole of public authority—the progressive aspects of colonial politics evoked in others an obverse fear that was no less compelling, no less a function of inherited ideas playing on an unstable polity. To crown representatives everywhere, and often to executives who were not direct agents of the crown, the extremism of opposition groups that could not be controlled by "influence" could be interpreted only as the result of the deliberate though dissembled efforts of factious demagogues to stir up an

[36] So John Adams translated the popular motto in 1775 (*Works,* C. F. Adams, ed., Boston, 1850–56, IV, 43)—an improvement, stylistically at least, over Arthur Lee's "suppress the disease in its infancy." *Virginia Gazette,* March 31, 1768.
[37] *Essay upon the Government of the English Plantations,* p. 36. Cf. *New York Weekly Journal,* Jan. 21, 1733[/34].

undiscriminating "democracy" to overthrow the balance of the constitution and engross the whole of the public authority. And further: since the links to England lay through the first and second orders of the colonial constitutions, the threat of constitutional disbalance in favor of the democracy involved by definition the threat of a severance of ties with England. Destruction of the constitutional balance would lead to mob rule, and that, in turn, to independence.

The fear of this conjoined catastrophe—anarchy and independence, both resulting naturally from the disbalancing of the constitution in favor of the third order of society—fills the pages of the correspondence of the governors with English officials from the earliest years of the eighteenth century, in terms that are indistinguishable from those that would be used in more celebrated circumstances in the 1760's and 1770's.[38] Illustrations could be drawn from almost any colony at almost any time in the century in situations where the first order of the constitution was faced with uncontrollable political opposition. So Governor Clinton believed in 1747 that the opposition in the New York Assembly

could only proceed from the most malicious spirit of wicked men whose design it was to wrest the King's authority out of the hands of his officers and to place the administration in a popular faction . . . The opposition of the faction proceeded from two motives: first, the desire of some ambitious men to put the government entirely in their own hands, which was the easier

[38] Cf. Bailyn, *Ideological Origins,* pp. 150–158.

to be accomplished as the majority of the Council and Assembly were ignorant, illiterate people of republican principles who had no knowledge of the English constitution or love for their country; secondly, from a design to establish a neutrality between the province of New York and Canada . . . whereby the enemy was supplied with provisions and the people of New York exposed to their ravages.[39]

But then, Clinton was incompetent and a neurotic. Governor Sharpe and Secretary Cecilius Calvert of Maryland were neither, yet they agreed in 1760 that a "madness of popular fury" had overtaken the commons of the province, and threatened to "overturn the whole frame of the constitution and throw everything into the hands of the People." They were by no means the first in that colony to say so. Twenty-five years earlier Governor Ogle had interpreted the Assembly's dismissal of placemen from its membership in the same terms. Six months before that, in 1733, the Board of Trade had informed the Privy Council that in Massachusetts the refusal of the Assembly to obey its native-born governor, Jonathan Belcher, "evidently shows that their design is to assume to themselves the executive power of the government of the said province and has a direct tendency to throw off their dependence upon Great Britain." Anarchic republicanism was endemic, it seemed, in that colony: "any man that behaves anything different from the crowd, stinks of the prerogative," one official reported

[39] *Documents Relative to the Colonial History of New York,* VI, 670, 671.

in 1730, an expression, he explained, that was "common with them"; it had not surprised him, he added, to discover certain leading politicians in Massachusetts circulating the rumor that the King and Queen had been poisoned and England once again caught up in civil war. A year earlier, in 1729, Newcastle, after reading reports on the state of affairs in Massachusetts, wrote to the already defeated—indeed, the already deceased—Governor Burnet that he agreed that there was "too much reason to think that the main drift of the Assembly . . . is to throw off their dependence on the crown." The question, a Board of Trade report of the same year insisted, "is not barely whether the people of the Massachusetts Bay shall give their governor a salary, nor even in what manner they ought to give it, but whether their repeated refusals upon this head compared with the whole course of their conduct for many years past does not manifestly tend to the throwing off their dependence upon the crown." Eight years earlier the Massachusetts agent Jeremiah Dummer in his *Defence of the New-England Charters* published the warning which he had earlier written privately to Massachusetts, that "people of all conditions and qualities" in England were saying of the charter colonies "that their increasing numbers and wealth joined to their great distance from Britain will give them an opportunity in the course of some years to throw off their dependence on the nation and declare themselves a free state, if not curbed in time."[40] And a decade before

---

[40] W. H. Browne, *et al.*, eds., *Archives of Maryland* (Baltimore, 1883–), IX, 376, 377 (cf. p. 430: "the majority of

that, in 1712, Governor Hunter in New York had assured the secretary of state that he had done everything in the power of man to bring the Assembly of that colony to its senses: "But now the mask is thrown off; they have called in question the Council's share in the legislation, trumped up an inherent right, . . . and have but one short step to make towards what I am unwilling to name."[41]

Demagoguery, to crown officials, lurked everywhere, and behind it the threat of independence. Dissemblance of hidden, anti-constitutional motives alone could explain the persistence of opposition on the part of leaders who professed the innocence of their intentions but who nevertheless continued to block all efforts of the first order of the constitution to stabilize the rocketing factionalism. Governor Dobbs of North Carolina had ruefully to admit

---

the people who elect the Lower House [are] ignorant of the necessity of supporting government at all, being Levellers in their principles and impatient of rule"); XXXIX, 150; William N. Sainsbury, *et al.*, eds., *Calendar of State Papers, Colonial Series* . . . (London, 1860–), 1733, p. 101; 1730, p. 120; 1728–29, pp. 413, 585; Jeremiah Dummer, *Defence of the New-England Charters* (London, 1731), pp. 60–61 (cf. Dummer to [? Sec. Willard], London, April 8, 1720, in *Collections of the Massachusetts Historical Society*, 3rd ser., I, 144–145, warning that people in England "fancy us to be a little kind of sovereign state, and conclude for certain that we shall be so in time to come, and that the crown will not be able to reduce us at so great a distance from the throne").

41 *Documents Relative to the Colonial History of New York*, V, 296. For Hunter's reliance on James Harrington's idiosyncratic formulation in explaining that New York, whose assembly was "claiming all the privileges of a House of Commons and stretching them even beyond what they were ever imagined to be there," was moving from "provincial or dependent empire" to "national or independent empire," see Bailyn, *Ideological Origins*, p. 75n.

that he had been duped by the Assembly leader John Starkey; everything about him had been persuasive: "his capacity and diligence . . . his garb and seeming humility, by wearing shoe strings, a plain coat, and having a bald head . . . but [he] is the most designing man in the province . . . He is a professed violent republican, in every instance taking from His Majesty's prerogative and encroaching upon the rights of the Council and adding to the power of the Assembly to make himself popular." There was no easy way, Dobbs explained, of penetrating immediately the pretenses of such dissembling demagogues as Starkey. Their secret purposes were characteristically so disguised, so masked, as to appear, until it was too late, indistinguishable from true patriotism.[42] "The common run of the species," the *New York Mercury* declared in 1755, was so easily tricked: they

> seldom examine things with attention . . . Let but a crafty designing imposter employ a herd of sycophants to blazon his reputation and trumpet his fame, and 'tis odds if he prove not more successful and popular than the real patriot, who confides in his own innocence and contents himself with doing good for the sake of goodness . . . Indeed, the people are so liable to be imposed upon by false shows and artful pretenses that we are not always to look upon their favor as the badge of true patriotism and a truly public spirit: on the contrary, we shall find that it is often acquired by sinister methods in order to carry on some crafty and sinister design . . . A little attention to the subdolous artifices of those pretended patriots would soon have discovered

[42] *Colonial Records of North Carolina*, V, 948.

those darlings, those revered guides of theirs, to have been their most pestilent enemies, wolves in sheeps' clothing.[43]

The result of continued inattention to such "subdolous artifices" was not hard to see. If some way were not found of stamping out opposition, Thomas Penn declared, "the constitution will be changed to a perfect democracy," which, he said, "must not be." But the threat persisted, and fed the fears which, Lieutenant Governor Clarke of New York said in 1741, had "for some years . . . obtained in England, that the plantations [were] not without thoughts of throwing off their dependence on the crown of England." How formidable were the combined dangers of democracy and independence need not be left to the imagination, the Reverend Andrew Eliot wrote his valued correspondent, the libertarian propagandist Thomas Hollis, in 1767; its horrible consequences had long been manifest, in that hopeless bedlam, Rhode Island, where, Eliot wrote, "they are divided into furious parties; they bribe, they quarrel, they hardly keep from blows. The parties are so nearly equal that they change governors and magistrates almost every year. If things are so bad in that little government, what would they be in greater? I hope not to live to see the American British colonies disconnected from Great Britain."[44]

43 *New York Mercury*, March 3, 1755.
44 William S. Hanna, *Benjamin Franklin and Pennsylvania Politics* (Stanford, 1964), p. 171; Smith, *History of the Late Province of New-York*, II, 53; Eliot to Hollis, Dec. 10, 1767, in *Collections of the Massachusetts Historical Society*, 4th ser., IV, 420–421.

But by then—1767—when Eliot was writing, politics in America had entered a new phase—or so it appears in the standard compartmentalization of American history. By then the train of events that manifestly led to Independence was clearly visible: Stamp Act, Townshend Duties, Massacre. But these enactments and the other famous events of the period are not self-evidently incendiary. The stamp tax was not a crushing tax; it was generally considered to be an innocuous and judicious form of taxation. The Townshend Duties, which were also far from crippling, were withdrawn. And the Massacre was the result of a kind of urban riot common both in England and America throughout the century. Yet these events were in fact incendiary; they did in fact lead to the overthrow of constituted authority and, ultimately, to the transformation of American life. For they were not in some pure sense simply objective events, and they were not perceived by immaculate minds aloft in a cosmic perch. To minds steeped in the literature of eighteenth-century history and political theory, these events, charged with ideology, were the final realization of tendencies and possibilities that had been seen and spoken of, with concern and foreboding, since the turn of the seventeenth century. There was no calm before the storm. The storm was continuous, if intermittent, throughout the century. An inflamed, unstable politics, incapable of duplicating the integration and control that "influence" had created in England, had called forth the full range of advanced ideas, not as theories simply, not as warnings merely of some ultimate potentiality, but as explanations of present conflicts, bitter conflicts, conflicts between a legally overgreat executive and an irrepressible though shifting opposition. What in England were theoretical dangers decried by an extremely vocal but politically harmless opposition, appeared in the colonies to be real dangers that threatened an actual and not a theoretical disbalancing of the mixed constitution in favor of an executive engrossment, with all the evils that were known to follow from that destructive event. Obversely, the possibility that lurked within every mixed constitution, that the force of "the democracy" would overreach its proper boundaries and encroach upon the area of power properly entrusted to the first order of the constitution, seemed continuously to be at the edge of realization. Both fears seemed realistic; neither merely theoretical; neither merely logical.

But if American politics through the eighteenth century was latently revolutionary in this sense—if in these ways the pattern of ideas that would give transcendent meaning to the events of the 1760's and 1770's was already present decades earlier—the ultimate dangers had nevertheless been averted. For before 1763 there had been no relentless pressures within the system of Anglo-American politics, no sustained drive or inescapable discipline guided by central policy. When, after the conclusion of the Seven Years' War, that impetus and control appeared in the form of a revamped colonial system with more effective agencies of enforcement; when the system finally tightened and the pressure was maintained; and when, associated with this, evidence accumulated in the colonies that corruption was softening the vigilance that had heretofore preserved England's own mixed constitution—that an escalation of ministerial power initially stimulated by John Stuart, Earl of Bute, was taking place in England itself—when all of this happened, the latent tendencies of American politics moved swiftly to their ultimate fulfillment.

INDEX

INDEX

Board of Trade, 74, 76, 82, 91, 120, 154, 155

Bohemia, 151

Bolingbroke, Viscount: *see* St. John, Henry

Borgia, Caesar, 138

Boston, 59, 98, 111, 115, 116, 145

Boston Evening Post, 140, 145

Boston Gazette, 54, 145

Boston Massacre, 12, 159

Boston Weekly News Letter, 60, 145

Bradford, William, 141

Braintree (Mass.), 98

Bristol (England), 100

Britain: *see* England

British empire, 8, 9, 10

British Journal, 40

Brooke, John, 25–6

Brown, John: *Estimate . . . of the Times*, 51, 55

Brutus, 148

Burgh, James: *Britain's Remembrancer*, 51, 55

Burke, Edmund, 100, 127; Speech to the Electors of Bristol 84–5

Burnet, Bishop Gilbert, 110, 141

Burnet, William, 61, 110–11, 115, 116, 134, 155

Burrington, George, 120, 137

Bute, Earl of: *see* Stuart, John

Byrd, William, II, 139; see also *Essay upon the Government of the English Plantations*

Caesar, Julius, 138, 140, 148

Calvert, Cecilius, 77, 154

Calvert, Frederick, 7th Earl of Baltimore, 62

Cambridge (Mass.), 98

Campbell, Alexander: *Maxima Libertatis Custodia . . .*, 146

Canada, 93, 154; trade of, 94, 110–11, 112

Canterbury, Archbishop of, 112

Caribbean islands: *see* West Indies

Catholics, 84

Cato, 55

Cato: see Addison, Joseph

Cato's Letters: see Trenchard, John

Charles I, 111, 115, 118, 147; *Answer to the XIX Propositions*, 20, 61

Charles II, 55, 141, 147

Chartists, 68

Chelsea (England), 32

Church of England, 94–5; relation of, to the state, 24–5

Churchill, John, 1st Duke of Marlborough, 34, 108

Cicero, Marcus Tullius, 19

Clarendon, Earl of: *see* Hyde, Edward

Clarke, George, 113, 158

Clinton, George, 112, 113, 127, 136, 153, 154

Coercive Acts, 12

Colden, Cadwallader, 108, 131

Commons, 21, 24, 48, 56; constitutional role of, 22–23; British fear of, in colonies, 152–8; *see also* Democracy

ii

Index

Index

INDEX

Narragansett Bay, 99
Navigation acts, 71
Neville, Henry, 39
New England, 14, 94, 116; election sermons, 144
New England Courant, 54, 130, 138
New Hampshire, 68, 88, 92, 94, 123–4
New Jersey, 75, 78, 112
New York: 55, 56, 84, 95, 97–8, 104, 107, 116, 117, 131, 132, 134, 146, 158; Septennial Act, 68; judges' salaries in, 75; Assembly of, 80, 107–8, 109, 110, 113, 114, 128, 131, 153–4, 156; franchise in, 87; factionalism in, 107–14; Council of, 131, 154, 156; *see also* DeLancey family; Morrisite faction; Leislerians; Presbyterian Party
New York Gazette, 125–6, 128
New York Gazette Revived in the Weekly Post-Boy, 127, 128
New York Mercury, 56, 129, 145, 150, 157, 158
New York Weekly Journal, 54, 98, 117, 137, 138, 152
Newcastle, Duke of: *see* Pelham-Holles, Thomas
Nicholson, Sir Francis, 123, 137
Nobility, 23; *see also* Aristocracy
Nonconformity, 25; *see also* Protestant Dissenting Deputies
Norris, Isaac, 55

North Carolina, 76, 87, 120–121, 156–7
Norwich (England), 16
Nott, Edward, 122

O Liberty, Thou Goddess Heavenly Bright . . . , 80
Ogle, Samuel, 154
Oliver, Peter: *Origin . . . of the American Revolution*, 5
Opposition: not faction, 37–38; literature of English, in America, 38–9, 53, 54 ff.; view of society, 48–52; in free government, 126; *see also* England; Faction; Government; Parliament; Party
Orkney, Earl of: *see* Hamilton, James
Osborn, Sir Danvers, 113
Osborne, Thomas, 1st Earl of Danby, 33
Osgood, Herbert L., 9
Otis, James, Jr., 4, 5
Otis family, 98

Paley, William: *Principles of Moral and Political Philosophy*, 73
Pares, Richard, 101–2
Paris, Ferdinand John, 92–3
Parke, Daniel, 137
Parliament: House of Commons, 8, 20, 23, 24, 28, 63, 68, 78, 81, 122, 132, 133; House of Lords, 20, 22, 24, 61, 131, 132, 133; relation of, to King, 24–5; management and voting of,

BERNARD BAILYN was born in Hartford, Connecticut, in 1922. He was graduated from Williams College in 1945 and received his A.M. (1947) and Ph.D. (1953) degrees from Harvard University. He has taught at Harvard since 1949, becoming professor in 1961, and Winthrop Professor of History in 1966. He is editor-in-chief of the John Harvard Library and co-editor of *Perspectives in American History*. His other books include *The New England Merchants in the Seventeenth Century; Massachusetts Shipping, 1697–1714; Education in the Forming of American Society; Pamphlets of the American Revolution;* and *The Ideological Origins of the American Revolution*.

VINTAGE POLITICAL SCIENCE
AND SOCIAL CRITICISM